Camcorder in the Classroom
Using the Videocamera to
Enliven Curriculum

Adrienne L. Herrell
California State University, Fresno

Joel P. Fowler, Jr.
California State University, Fresno

Prentice Hall
Upper Saddle River, New Jersey   Columbus, Ohio

Library of Congress Cataloging-in-Publication Data

Herrell, Adrienne L.
    Camcorder in the classroom : using the videocamera to enliven
curriculum / Adrienne L. Herrell, Joel P. Fowler, Jr.
        p.   cm.
    Includes bibliographical references and index.
    ISBN 0-13-591280-6
    1. Video tapes in education—United States.   2. Camcorders.
I. Fowler, Joel P.   II. Title.
LB1044.75.H47   1998
371.33'523—DC21

97-34197
CIP

Editor: Debra A. Stollenwerk
Production Editor: Christine Harrington
Text Designer, Illustrations, and Production Coordinator: Custom Editorial Productions, Inc.
Design Coordinator: Karrie M. Converse
Cover Designer: Proof Positive/Farrowlyne Assoc., Inc.
Production Manager: Laura Messerly
Director of Marketing: Kevin Flanagan
Marketing Manager: Suzanne Stanton
Advertising/Marketing Coordinator: Julie Shough

This book was set in Leawood and Benguiat Gothic by Custom Editorial Productions, Inc., and was printed and bound by Book Press. The cover was printed by Phoenix Color Corp.

© 1998 by Prentice-Hall, Inc.
Simon & Schuster/A Viacom Company
Upper Saddle River, New Jersey 07458

Photo credits: Colin Bateman, p. 129; Joel Fowler, pp. 17, 147; Adrienne Herrell, pp. 3, 29, 61, 64, 83, 96, 107

Printed in the United States of America

10 9 8   7 6 5 4 3 2 1

ISBN 0-13-591280-6

Prentice-Hall International (UK) Limited, *London*
Prentice-Hall of Australia Pty. Limited, *Sydney*
Prentice-Hall Canada, Inc., *Toronto*
Prentice-Hall Hispanoamericana, S. A., *Mexico*
Prentice-Hall of India Private Limited, *New Delhi*
Prentice-Hall of Japan, Inc., *Tokyo*
Simon & Schuster Asia Pte. Ltd., *Singapore*
Editora Prentice-Hall do Brasil, Ltda., *Rio de Janeiro*

To Gail E. Tompkins, the consummate colleague
—A. L. H.

To Marilyn, a classroom teacher, and to classroom teachers everywhere who give much of themselves so that children may learn and, perhaps, teach others.
—J. P. F.

The use of video technology in classrooms across the United States varies widely. In some areas every school has a video production lab with multiple camcorders, digital editing equipment, and closed-circuit television wired into every classroom. In other parts of the country, many schools are just becoming aware of the power of school-made videos and are either purchasing their first equipment or bringing it out of the closet and dusting it off.

Although they have been using commercially produced teaching videos for a number of years, many teachers have never felt confident enough to produce their own videos in the classroom. Because we believe that video cameras can make a major impact on the effectiveness and motivation to learn in classrooms, this book was written to support teachers, kindergarten through college, in the use of this fascinating technology.

THE PURPOSE OF THIS BOOK

Our purpose in writing this book is to make video production a reality in the classroom. It is intended to demonstrate ways in which teachers in elementary, middle, and high schools, as well as in college, can use the camcorder and VCR to teach and motivate their students and assess their progress. Our intention is not to make expert video producers of the teachers and students but to show ways in which curriculum can be enlivened by the addition of video. We give you simple steps to get you started using a camcorder in the classroom and video practice activities that lead you through steps to become more proficient in video use.

Chapter 1 introduces the reader to the equipment and very basic techniques needed to begin to make effective classroom video. The following chapters are written for particular curriculum applications. If you are a high school math teacher, you will want to read Chapters 1 and 3. Elementary teachers will find a wealth of ideas across the curriculum. Obviously, our suggestions will not be all-encompassing. Once you have started using this fascinating medium, you will find many more uses in the classroom and beyond.

Appendix A, Video Resources, provides information of interest to readers who want to move beyond the basics of video production. Appendix B, Teacher Resource, provides sources for information about related fields such as copyright laws, television literacy, and support for expanded implementation of video in the classroom.

THE CHAPTER FORMAT

Each chapter is formatted to give you an advance organizer. By reading the short vignette and chapter objectives, you will be prepared to understand what the material in the chapter will teach. Each chapter provides a video practice activity that involves you in practicing new techniques with the camcorder and gradually moves you into more difficult applications, chapter by chapter. In addition, each chapter will give you suggestions for evaluating, refining, and improving the videos that you make.

Involving the student in making classroom videos can be very motivating. Suggestions for ways that the students themselves can use this technology are included in every chapter. Also in each chapter you will find suggestions for involving parents.

All of the suggestions made in this book have been field-tested in classrooms across the United States. Many of the suggestions came from classroom teachers who are excited about using the camcorder in the classroom and the results they obtain with their students.

In researching this book, we have seen motivated students in California, Florida, Texas, and New Hampshire who know how to use the techniques we have described for teachers. If the kids can do it, so can we! We learned this about computers, and we see it happening with camcorders. There is probably a camcorder gathering dust in a closet somewhere in your school, so dust it off and join the new generation of technology.

CONTENTS

1

Using the Camcorder in the Classroom

Getting in the Video Mode

Susan and John are both primary grade teachers. They are sitting in the teacher's lounge at their elementary school discussing the upcoming Back-to-School Night.

"I wish I could find a way to demonstrate to the parents all the innovations we are using in education today," says Susan.

"We've had such great success with our Reading/Writing Workshop," says John. "But when I try to explain it to parents, all I get is raised eyebrows. They seem to think of it as controlled chaos."

Claudia enters the lounge just as John is speaking and interjects, "I just finished making a videotape of my Reading/Writing Workshop. I'm going to show it at Back-to-School Night so the parents will see how much reading and writing goes on in a classroom today."

John looks surprised. "Isn't that a lot of work?"

Claudia grins. "I just walked around during the workshop time today and asked children to show their work and talk about it. They read brief sections of their writing and we discussed ways that they could make it more interesting or descriptive. It wasn't that different from my regular approach."

John looks doubtful. "Aren't video cameras expensive?"

"The price is going down all the time. I bought a video camera for home," replies Claudia. "Now I can use it both at home and school. Come down to the room and I'll show you how easy it is to use. The new ones are really almost foolproof, and they've gotten a lot less expensive, too."

"But won't we need a lot of expensive editing equipment too?" asks John as he and Susan follow Claudia out of the lounge.

1

"I use a technique called in-camera editing for the tapes I'm making," Claudia replies. "They turn out pretty well. I'm getting better with every tape I make."

Susan suggests, "Let's invite Mr. Ottman to see how well your video works at Back-to-School Night and maybe he'll buy a camera for the school."

John chuckles, "If it helps the parents to understand the new approaches to teaching reading and writing, he'll probably be GLAD to buy a video camera!"

Claudia agrees, "This is exciting! I want to make a tape about inventive spelling to show the parents how well it works to get children excited about writing."

"Great idea!" add Susan and John.

Meanwhile, at Washington High School across town, Charles, the principal; Marie, the Latin Club sponsor; and Alicia, the media specialist, are discussing the lack of participation in academic-related clubs on campus.

Marie says, "The students in Latin Club are all active in a number of other activities, but their Latin is going to serve them well on college entrance exams. I wish I could get them to realize that academic club members aren't all 'nerds.'"

Charles smiles, "I was a Latin Club member myself and took a lot of kidding from the rest of my football team. What can we do to publicize the clubs in a more appealing light?"

Alicia suggests, "Why don't we make a video to show at orientation? We could feature the academic clubs and show that the members aren't all nerds. We also can provide some up-beat background music and highlight the benefits of belonging to these types of clubs. This type of video isn't hard to make."

"Wonderful idea!" replies Charles. "Can you two work on this?"

"Of course," smiles Marie. "My students will be delighted to be television stars. How many other academic clubs are there?"

"Let's see." says Alicia, "There's Spanish, French, Chess, Debate."

Charles slips out of the lounge quietly with a smile on his face.

Teachers working together can support each other in the use of camcorders in their classrooms.

CHAPTER OBJECTIVES

As John, Claudia, Susan, Charles, Marie, and Alicia are discovering, cameras can be used in the classroom in many ways. By reading this chapter and completing the video practice activity, you will learn

1. Some ways in which your students will benefit from the use of the camcorder in the classroom.
2. The basic information you need to begin making simple video montages in your classroom.
3. Ways to avoid the most common mistakes made by beginning videographers.
4. Ways to add simple audio to your videotapes.

WHY USE VIDEO IN THE CLASSROOM?

Much of the recent research in learning and motivation suggests that students are more motivated to learn when they have ways to become actively engaged in the learning process (Graves,1995; Hepler, 1991; Staab, 1991). Learning theory also tells us that an integrated approach to learning helps to engage learners from multiple perspectives (Gardner, 1993; Caine & Caine, 1991). Video production in the classroom involves teachers and students in a variety of ways. The topic of the video to be made can be anything from a reenactment of literature to documenting a science experiment to capturing an athletic or creative arts production on tape. The planning that is required to make good video productions involves time and collaboration, but the teachers and students involved are using a variety of curricular areas as well as multiple intelligences (Gardner, 1993). The writing of a script for a video production combined with the planning of shot sequences and prop and scenery needs encourages the use of reading, writing, speaking, listening, artistic, interpersonal, spatial, and logical-mathematical skills. Gardner's research on multiple intelligences shows that students who are able to use their strong intelligences to learn and to demonstrate their understanding become more engaged in learning activities and benefit more in terms of concept development and understanding. All of the seven intelligences identified by Gardner's research (linguistic, logical-mathematical, spatial, musical, kinesthetic, interpersonal, and intrapersonal) are involved in video planning and production. All students have an opportunity to become engaged in a way that is most compatible with their strong intelligences, as well as experiences to enhance their weaker ones.

> Video production provides the ultimate opportunity for student engagement in learning. It is by definition integrated in nature involving script writing, artistic rendering, oral presentation, and technical knowledge and application.

USE OF VIDEO IN SCHOOLS

Video has been used for documenting athletic and artistic endeavors for a number of years, but classroom teachers have typically used camcorders only to record play productions and other "major events" (Nourie, 1990). The type of videotaping teachers usually do requires very little expertise or advanced planning. The teacher simply sets up the camcorder on a tripod and tapes the performance, occasionally zooming in or out at specific points. The use of camcorders in classrooms and school is now beginning to move beyond this type of videotaping into more creative applications. Across the country, teachers are discovering more innovative uses of the camcorder.

- In many schools, a video production group or class produces and presents a morning newscast for the entire school.
- Teachers are using the camcorder to produce videos to share with parents in which they explain curriculum being taught in the classroom and ways that the parents can support their child's learning.
- Students are writing and producing documentaries about specific times in history or particular historical events.
- Teachers are videotaping guest speakers or field trips for use in review and discussion.
- Students of foreign languages are viewing tapes of their own communications and conversations for review and critique.
- Students of all ages are producing videos of updated versions of literary classics.
- Teachers are videotaping students as they do oral presentations, book reports, debates, and speeches and are including the videotapes in the student portfolios.
- Students are including a video of themselves in their letters to penpals within the school, across town, or across the country.

The list of innovative uses of video in the classroom goes on and on. Some school districts have included television studios in plans for new buildings and are actually teaching video production classes. Other schools have started in a small way by purchasing a single camcorder and VCR. The main factor in whether video is used in the classroom is the teacher's level of comfort with the medium as well as willingness to invest the time to plan and work with students in producing video (Beasley, 1993).

Becoming familiar with the camcorder is the first step in getting teachers and students involved. Curriculum applications are many and varied, but teachers must gain confidence in their abilities to use this technology before they move to the next step, involving the students in planning and producing.

LEARNING THE VOCABULARY

Certain terms used in video production help you to communicate with your students, parents, and others involved in making the videos. Students are excited about learning and using the new vocabulary, and using it helps them to learn how language enables people to communicate about new things they are learning. The terms are introduced as the process of videotaping becomes a part of your classroom.

Stages of Production

Your video project will be divided into three stages: preproduction, production, and postproduction. *Preproduction* is everything that happens before the actual taping of the video. This is the most important phase of the process; it is when the basic ideas and approaches of the production are developed and set in motion. The success of your production rests primarily on the careful thought and detailed planning done in the preproduction stage. The script is written in preproduction, the shot sequences are planned out, the storyboards are drawn, and the decisions about where to tape are made.

Production is the stage in which the actual taping of the video sequence is done. The script and storyboards are followed, and rewrites are made as they become necessary. If in-camera editing is being used, this stage also includes viewing the shots as they are made to determine whether editing is necessary before new scenes are recorded.

Postproduction is the stage in which editing is typically done if traditional editing equipment is being used. Voice-over music and sound effects and graphics can also be added at this stage if the necessary equipment is available.

A SIMPLE BEGINNING

This book is not intended to turn classroom teachers into professional video producers. Its goal is instead to provide introductory strategies in producing video and exercises to help students and teachers become comfortable with using the camcorder and discovering curriculum that includes the use of video in teaching, motivating, and assessing students.

The first step in learning to use the camcorder in the classroom is to locate a camcorder and a tripod. Chances are that at least one of each of these is tucked away in a closet in your school. If not, try calling the district audiovisual resource library. If you have the opportunity to purchase a new camcorder, a section in Appendix A, Video Resources will assist you in making an informed selection.

Many school districts have video production resource teachers available to help you learn to use the camcorder and editing equipment. If your district doesn't have this kind of support, do not give up. Camcorders are not difficult to use; as with other technology, they just take practice.

Once you locate a camcorder and tripod, you need to become familiar with them and practice some simple videotaping. Camcorders differ, but most have standard features which are shown in Figure 1.1. You will begin by plugging in the power cord or inserting the battery, turning the camcorder on, and inserting a videotape. Practice taping for a few minutes to get the feel of the camera. Locate the power switch and the zoom buttons and simply experiment with the camera. You may find that it is difficult to hold the camera steady, which is why the tripod becomes necessary. Find the large screw on the head of the tripod, match it with the hole in the bottom of the camcorder, and attach the camcorder to the tripod. Before you let go, make sure that the camera is firmly attached. Adjust the height of the tripod so you can look through the camera viewfinder comfortably. It is important that the camera is located on the tripod so that it is level. Some tripods actually have a level attached; if not you'll have to "eyeball it." Your shots will be at an angle if the camcorder is not level.

Composition

If you are videotaping people or objects for TV, certain composition elements are important to remember so that when your videotape is played back on any size screen, your images are very similar to the way you had originally framed them in the

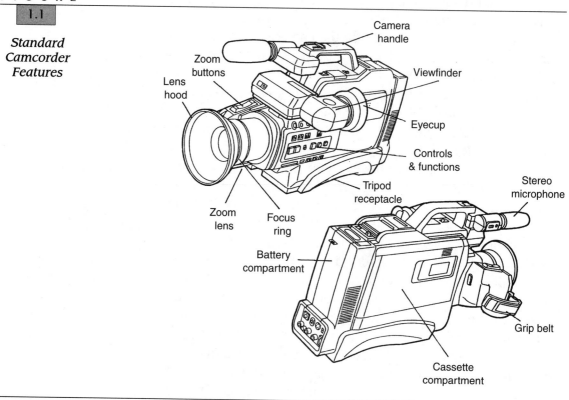

camera. Figure 1.2 shows some of the important aspects of composition: head room, and lead room.

Head Room

You will be shooting people on videotape more than any other subject. You need to make sure that when they are being framed in the viewfinder, you leave a slight space above their heads, called *head room*. Framing a person with the head "nudging" the top of the viewfinder tends to make the viewer unconsciously uncomfortable after a period of time. It also makes an unattractive picture. Take care, however, not to leave too much space above the head, which results in framing that is as unpleasing as not having enough room. Generally, the further the subject is from the camera, the more headroom is needed; the reverse is true for close-up shots.

F I G U R E   *Important Aspects of Composition*

1.2

Head Room

Too little head room

Too much head room

Correct head room

Head room should increase with longer shots

Lead Room

Too little lead room

Better

Correct

Too little lead room

Correct

Lead Room

The camera operator should always provide some look space—nose or eye room—by framing a subject with some space in front of him or her. This is also known as *lead room* since the object of the space is to lead the viewer into the imaginary next frame—in the direction the person in the shot is looking. Lead room is especially useful when you are shooting a moving subject, such as a person walking. By shooting slightly ahead in the direction the person is walking, you are again taking the viewer with you and keeping the action interesting.

Shot Size

The *shot* is the basic camera composition of images. Shots range from extreme long to extreme close-up and, in some instances, "pixel" close: focusing on an eye or hand, for example.

Extreme long shots (ELS) are used for the widest establishing shot to give the viewer an opportunity to see all the related elements in a shot and to establish the place in the mind, "Oh, this is taking place at school."

A *long shot (LS)* gives a little less of the overall picture than an ELS gives and usually provides viewers with a relationship of main people and the environment or setting.

A *medium shot* (MS) begins to close in on the principals and still includes some of the related environment or surroundings.

A *medium close-up (MCU)* is perhaps the most used shot for people in TV. Also known as a *chest shot* or a *head and shoulders shot*, it is the shot composition that is traditional in shooting news anchors. The surrounding area becomes secondary in importance.

A *close-up (CU)* is the shot responsible for TV being called the "close-up medium." It is the shot that generally features the human face in great detail. It is a dramatic shot, full of impact, and is used to show emotion and reaction. It can include the top of the head to the bottom of the chin.

An *extreme close-up: (ECU)* is used only for the most dramatic scenes. The focal points are the eyes and the nose but can sometimes include part of the chin. It is usually framed at midpoint in the forehead to right under the lower lip. Figure 1.3 shows examples of these shots.

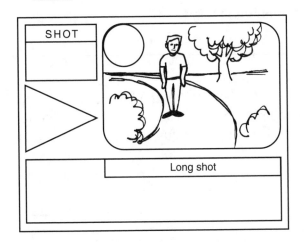

SHOT

Long shot

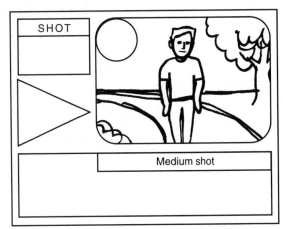

SHOT

Medium shot

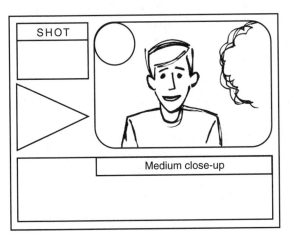

SHOT

Medium close-up

SHOT

Close-up

SHOT

Extreme close-up

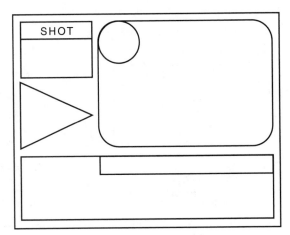

SHOT

Composing with Backgrounds in Mind

When you are framing a person in a shot, you are most likely doing it to focus viewers' attention on that person. Therefore, you do not want anything to detract from that focal point. When you are framing in the viewfinder, be very watchful of the area behind the person: other people whose activities may be distracting, busy designs on a wall or unusual furniture, surfaces above that may be in a line that falls directly on top of the person's head, and a tree branch, a lamp, or a telephone pole that seems to grow out of the top of a person's head. Any of these backgrounds can be enough of a distraction to cause the viewer to miss important messages being delivered by the principal subject. A slight change of camera position usually takes care of these composition problems. Figure 1.4 shows some examples of composition.

The Tripod

Until you have had plenty of practice with hand-holding camcorders, it is wise to use a *tripod* for most shoots. A *tripod* is a three-legged stand to which you attach the camcorder. Tripods allow for steady and smooth shots; they can be moved from place to place with the camera attached if you use care. See Figure 1.5, which shows the typical parts of a tripod.

F I G U R E   *Examples of Background Composition*
1.4

Background distracting

Background distracting

Background shows depth

FIGURE

1.5

A Typical Tripod

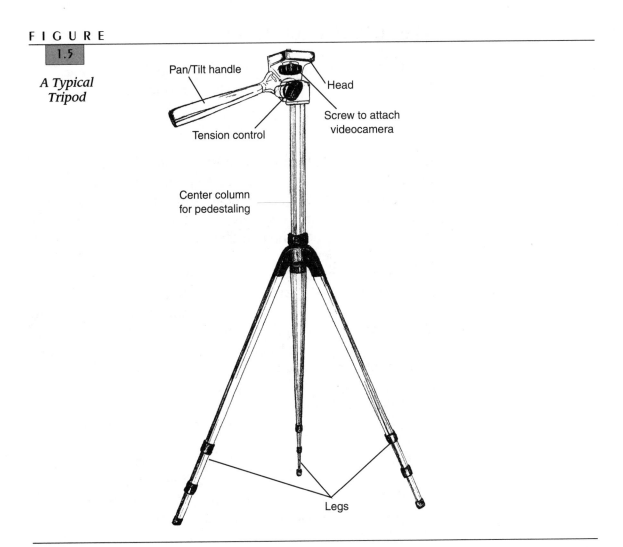

Pan/Tilt handle

Head

Screw to attach videocamera

Tension control

Center column for pedestaling

Legs

If possible, purchase a tripod with a *fluid head;* it is more expensive than a *friction-head pod,* but the ease and smoothness of movement make it far superior. You may also want to purchase a tripod that can be adapted with wheels. Although the majority of your initial shoots will likely be static, some of them may become sophisticated enough to require *dollying, trucking,* and *arcing* for a more professional-looking production, and the wheels then are indispensable.

BASIC CAMERA MOVEMENTS

The basic camera movements that will be discussed are illustrated in Figure 1.6; they include the following:

- Pan
- Tilt
- Dolly
- Zoom
- Truck
- Arc

It should be noted here that almost without exception, camera
movements are the smoothest when performed on a tripod, or
on a special track to accommodate tripods and dollies. Handheld movements are certainly common, especially in news
gathering, but steady shots in these instances are the result of
practice and experience.

A *pan,* or *panning,* is *horizontal* movement of the camera
head (the body of the camera) whether it is mounted on a
tripod or is handheld. The pan is helpful when you want to
show continuous images of persons or objects that are side
by side or in a lateral configuration. The right or left pan
movement can be accomplished from a stationary position;
the camera operator simply pivots the camera right or left.
Short pans or full, 360 degree moves can be accomplished
without the operator's having to move from the shooting
point.

A *tilt,* or *tilting,* is the vertical—up and down—movement of
the camera head from a stationary position. This allows a steady
shot that begins with the camera lens pointed either up or down
and moving the camera downward or upward. A tilt shot can
show the relationship of student interest and reaction from a
desk following up to a blackboard or easel.

When panning or tilting, exaggerate the movements; in
other words, go slowly. For example, slow pans are particularly
important when shooting a group of students in group discussion. The camera may be on one person who is talking, and
then another student responds, and the camera begins a pan
over to that person. Often, there is an urge to get there quickly
with a rapid "swish pan," that results in a blurred image. Resist
the urge. Even if the person you are panning toward stops
speaking, instead of panning more, zoom out to include the
whole group and then try for the next speaker and then another

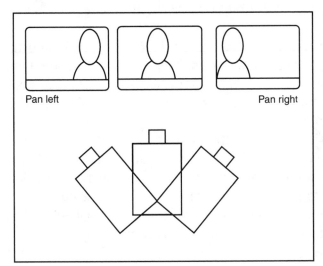

Pan left   Pan right

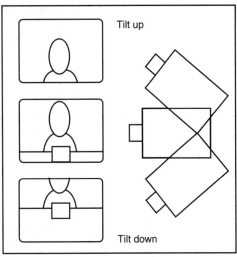

Tilt up

Tilt down

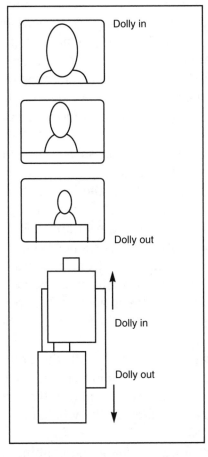

Dolly in

Dolly out

Dolly in

Dolly out

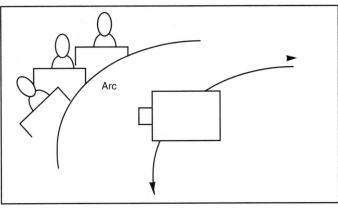

Arc

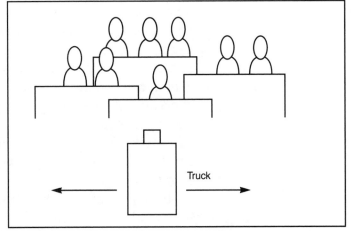

Truck

pan sequence. The only time you may want to speed up a pan or a tilt is for dramatic effect.

A *dolly* involves moving the entire camera, including the tripod, forward or backward or the operator who is handholding the camera physically moving in or out—from point A to point B. Some directors call for a "push in" or "push out" but, in effect are calling for a dolly shot.

In professional shoots, the camera is often mounted on a wheeled device—also called a *dolly*—that, in turn, rides on a track for maximum smoothness in the move. Fairly smooth dolly shots also have been accomplished while the camera operator is seated in a wheelchair or sitting in a wheeled desk chair being pushed by a production assistant.

Virtually all camcorders are equipped with zoom lenses. The zoom lens is controlled by servo buttons. The zoom movement is usually accomplished from a stationary camera by pushing the servo buttons marked T (for tight) and W (for wide). Whereas a dolly shot maintains the depth of field as it moves in or out, a zoom shot simply reduces or enlarges the size of the principal subject and either includes or excludes the objects in the space around the main subject as it moves backward or forward.

When preparing for zoom shots, make sure that your camera has been zoomed in to the tightest shot within the shooting area. Focus on that shot, and all of the images from the tightest to the widest will remain in focus for the full focal length of your shot. However, you must zoom in and refocus each time the camera is moved from its previous position. For example, if you needed to shoot a student in front of a blackboard, which had material that was important to the shot, *zoom in* and focus on the words on the board. If you *zoom out,* all persons and objects along that plane remain in focus until the zoom is ended.

A *truck* is a lateral, sideways, travel shot, with the entire camera and tripod being moved right or left. It is also known as a *crab movement.* The truck shot differs from a pan in that the depth of field in a truck shot is maintained as the whole unit—the tripod and camera—moves past the subjects.

An *arc* is a move that incorporates trucking and panning at the same time. The camera moves out from the subject, simul-

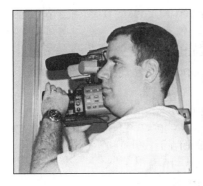  

Sometimes it is more convenient to rest the camera on the shoulder, on the knee or on a table in order to be more mobile or get a better angle.

taneously making a circular move, an arc, while panning and, sometimes, tilting to keep the subject in frame. The movement is used frequently in musical programs and in some dramatic presentations.

Whether you are shooting with a handheld camera or one mounted on a tripod, be aware that the *tighter* your shots (medium close-up to close-up), the smoother the camera movement needs to be. If your subject's features show up in close detail, so will even the slightest shake or wobble in the camera's movements. So when close shots are important to your production, try to use a tripod to keep your moving shots as smooth as possible.

Also try to vary the angle of your shots. Not all of your shooting needs to be from the teacher's viewpoint. As a rule, when the students are the principal subject, try to shoot from their perspective, their eye level. Most tripods allow for adjustments up or down. You can also choose a desk or table to rest the camera on and place items beneath the camera body (books, folded tissue, etc.) to frame all of the subject you need in the viewfinder.

Common Errors That Beginning Videographers Make

- Not using enough light
- Shooting into the light
- Panning and zooming too quickly

In the first practice activity you will make a video montage. This is simply a series of glimpses into a classroom or other setting. This gives you an opportunity to show parents and administrators an overview of your classroom day and the kinds of activities the children experience. This type of video is very useful for orientations and events such as Back-to-School Night. It is especially easy for an inexperienced videographer because you start at the beginning of the school day and videotape short sequences of activity periodically all day.

PRACTICE ACTIVITY

For middle school and high school teachers, choose a practice exercise that will be valuable to you in your setting. You could do a school orientation video, briefly showing the places and people in the school that a new student would need to know, or you can choose to do a video like the one described in the vignette at the beginning of the chapter, introducing clubs and activities available to the students.

Preproduction planning for the daily activities video is relatively simple. You have plans written for the day and you choose a few minutes of each activity to capture on videotape, selecting scenes that show student involvement and the variety of activities that occur during a typical school day. For the middle and high school video, you need to work with the sponsors of the clubs or the people who will be featured in the video. Explain what you want to accomplish and schedule a time to videotape them or the club activities. You will need to do the following:

- Make sure that you have a fresh videotape available.
- Make sure that the batteries are charged if you are using the camcorder battery pack.
- Prepare the students ahead of time so they understand the purpose of the videotape and resist the impulse to wave and say "Hi Mom!" every time the camera comes their way.
- Help them to plan walking routes in the classroom that allow them to avoid walking in front of the camera.
- Clear the aisles in the classroom as much as possible so you can move freely around as you tape.

You can provide an introductory visual for your video by showing a message written on the chalkboard or a poster made by the students identifying the classroom, grade level, and school. You don't have to have fancy graphics to make an effective video.

Tape short scenes from the classroom periodically throughout the day. Thirty-second glimpses are sufficient for most activities. View the sequences after you tape them to make sure that you got what you wanted and then rewind the tape to the place where you want to begin the next sequence. Some cameras have a built-in fade that allows you to move from scene to scene by fading to black or other visual. You can also try some innovative things such as starting a sequence focused on a student's school sweatshirt and gradually moving away from the student to show the larger scene. Other ways to move smoothly from scene to scene include these:

- Dropping a piece of construction paper in front of the lens, pausing the camera, and starting the next scene by focusing on the same piece of construction paper and then moving it away.
- Ending one scene by moving the lens close to a person or object in the classroom and then beginning the next scene by moving away from the same person or object.

- Providing student-made signs to use in identifying each segment. Examples include Reading Workshop, Physical Education, and Lunch.

After you have made the video montage, practice showing it and describing what is happening in the scenes. As you describe the scenes, audio tape what you say to use in writing a script to be added to the tape using the audio dub mechanism on the camcorder.

Creating the Script

View the montage, noting the exact length of time for each segment. List the scenes and times sequentially down the left side of a piece of paper divided into two columns. See Figures 1.7 and 1.8 for examples. On the right side of the paper, next to each video sequence, write the script for the scene. Read the script for each scene slowly and carefully, timing the delivery to make sure that it matches the time of the video scene. Do this for each of the scenes, including the introduction and final scene.

If you want to have a musical background, choose music that fits the mood of the video. In the Appendix B, Teacher Resource, you will find a list of resources for obtaining copyright-free music to use with your video productions.

Directions for Audio Dubbing the Music and Script

Once your videotape is complete, carefully time each segment. Make a copy of the videotape and practice the audio dubbing with the copy. Set the original tape aside until you are sure you have the audio dubbing timed out correctly.

Using a cassette tape recorder, record the musical background and the script on audiotape, timing the script reading carefully so that it will coincide with the video images on the videotape. Cue up the audio tape as precisely as you can on the cassette machine. Place the copy of the videotape into the camcorder and, using the cable and jack from the audio cassette machine, plug the jack into the audio accessory or external socket on the camcorder. Push the audio dub button on the camcorder, the record button, and play back the cassette tape.

If everything has worked properly with the audio dub function, the previously recorded audio on the videotape should have been erased and replaced with the new audio fed from the cassette machine into the camcorder. If it has performed to your satisfaction, you are now ready to dub the audio onto the previously videotaped original master videotape. If you need to make adjustments in the audio, make them and then try the dub again with the copy of the videotape before you dub the audio onto the original.

VIDEO PROJECT

Now that you have completed a practice video using the video montage approach, choose a video project that fits your needs and repeat the process. Project suggestions include the following:

FIGURE

	Video	Audio
1.7 *Script for First-Grade Parent Orientation*	Close-up of visual "Welcome to Room 2" :10	Welcome to Mrs. Brown's first grade, room 2.
	Children entering the room :08	The children arrive at school eager to start the day.
	Pledge of allegiance :06	We start the day in much the same way you did as a first grader. We still say the pledge to the flag and sing patriotic songs.
	Children reading library books :15	But when you come to visit our classroom, you will see that we do many things differently. We have free reading time every day. We get lots of chances to enjoy books.
	Teacher instructing at chalkboard :12	The instruction in first grade is done in small groups, and we do a lot of reading and writing.
	Children writing :08	Children begin to write their own books using temporary spelling. We value their thought and ideas and move them into conventional spelling gradually throughout the year.
	Lunchroom scene :06	After the morning of reading and writing, we go to lunch. Our cafeteria serves nutritious lunches.
	Recess scene :08	After lunch, we go outside for fresh air and exercise.
	Science experiment scene :10	We do a lot of experiments and hands-on activities in science. We learn about plants and animals in first grade.
	Math manipulatives scene :08	In math we learn to count, add, subtract, and solve problems. We use a lot of manipulatives to help us understand how math works.
	Read aloud scene :06	We enjoy having books read to us and like to reread books that our teacher has read.
	Interactive writing scene :08	One of the ways we learn to spell words and write sentences is called *interactive writing*. Our teacher helps us to use our phonics to listen to the sounds in words and spell them correctly.
	Children exiting the room :04	We work hard in first grade but sometimes we hate to go home.
	Child with big smile :04	School is fun!

FIGURE

1.8

*High School
Clubs
Orientation
Script*

Video	Audio
"Academic Clubs at Washington High School—Opportunities for Leadership"—sign :05	Clubs at Washington High School present many opportunities for student leadership.
Scenes of practice and inter-scholastic debates and awarding of trophies :20	Participating in debate club prepares us to think on our feet. Members compete in state and national debate tournaments and have won the state competition three out of the last four years. Did you know that 87% of all members of Congress participated in debate at the high school level?
Scenes of Latin Club meetings :20 Scene of Latin Club party :08	Latin Club helps us to really find ways to use the Latin we are learning to increase our English vocabulary and learn more about the great civilization of the Roman empire. Guest speakers help us to make connections between the Latin language and the history of the modern world. The end of the year toga party is great fun too.
Scene of Spanish Club Meetings :15 Scene of Spanish Club fiesta :12	Spanish club meetings are conducted in Spanish and give us a chance to refine our spoken fluency. Guests from the community present information about the arts and music of the Spanish-speaking world. The year-end participation in the Cinco de Mayo festival usually earns us enough for a field trip to Mexico and a chance to practice Spanish with native-speaking people and taste the sights and sounds of our neighbor to the south.
Scenes of French Club Meetings :15	French club meetings involve many activities to increase our French vocabulary and become more fluent. Games and debates in French are conducted with support from native speakers of French who are members of our community helping us to perfect our accents.
Scene of French Club field trip :12	Although we haven't taken a field trip to France, we do take field trips to local French restaurants, order our food in French, and converse in French for the evening.

FIGURE

	Video	Audio
1.8		
(continued)	Scene of Chess Club practice matches :12	Chess club is a club where we can learn to play chess or play at the competitive level. There is always someone to challenge us to higher levels of play. Chess competition is a part of club activities for those who are ready for it. Our club has won the state high school tournament twice in the past five years. Lessons are also available for beginning players.
	Scene of Chess Club in competition and accepting trophy :15	
	Brief scenes of academic club members in other roles Cheerleader :02 Band member :02 Football player :02 Student body president :02 Total time 2:22	The members of academic clubs at Washington High are very well-rounded students who cheer for our teams, play in our band, participate in varsity sports, and stand out as leaders of the school. Check the bulletin board outside the counselor's office for the days and times of meetings. All academic clubs are open to all students.

- A montage of the students in your class, shown in class and out, highlighting their unique interests and talents. Involve the students in writing the script that tells about them.
- An orientation montage of the school showing all the places and people the students need to know.
- An orientation montage about you, the teacher, your interests, talents, and beliefs about teaching.
- A montage showing outstanding work that your students have done to be used in introducing the parents and administrators to the products of your class.
- An introductory montage of exciting projects done in your class one year to be saved and shown to new students and parents in subsequent years so they can anticipate the kinds of learning activities the students will experience.
- A video showing important factors in developing good study skills, of a quiet place to study; of a place to store pencils, papers, dictionary; of a specific time set aside for homework; of a good reading lamp.
- A video showing opportunities for community service in your neighborhood.

- *For high school students,* show the steps in applying for college, preparing for job interviews, or preparing a resume.
- *For parents,* show reading to a child, getting involved in a child's education, or using television to keep the lines of communication open.

The following are important steps in creating useful video montages:

1. Choose a topic that will be useful in introducing your class, subject, or beliefs to the students or parents.
2. Keep the scenes short and lively.
3. Plan the scenes to flow smoothly. If you are taping a sequential montage, help the audience to recognize the sequence. If you are taping a series of students, have one student pass something to the next student or find a way to have the scenes flow.
4. Keep the script short and interesting and the music lively.

Reviewing and Refining Your Video

After you have completed a video, sit down and view it critically. Since you are just beginning, don't be overly critical, but think of things you can do in the next video to make it more professional. Think of the things you have learned about composition, head room, nose room, sequence, and flow. Jot down some notes to yourself so that you will remember to plan the areas of difficulty more carefully next time.

Involving the Parents

As you plan the video, think about things the parents can do to be more involved in their children's education. Showing a parent or older child reading individually with a student in the classroom should be used as an opportunity to invite the parents into the classroom as volunteers. Showing a parent demonstrating a hobby or teaching a lesson related to the parent's job can serve as an example of other ways that parents can be involved. If you are planning other videos to help keep the parents informed, mention this at Back-to-School Night and ask that the parents become involved in this project. They can let you know if there are topics that would be of interest to them, such as how to help a child with a science project or how to read stories to a child. Some parents might be interested in a video about the steps in the writing process or ways to interest an uninterested reader or writer. The more adept you get with your video camera, the more ways you will find to use video in home-school relations.

SUMMARY

The use of video in the classroom provides opportunities for students and teachers to become actively engaged in teaching and learning. Video production is by definition an integrated approach for which students and teachers must use their skills in language arts, visual arts, music, and technology and must collaborate.

Chapter 1 introduced the video montage as an approach to making simple videos for classroom use. The *video montage* is a sequence of scenes taped to create a visual image of a classroom, setting, or concept. The *preproduction phase* of this approach involves planning the sequence of scenes to be taped and ways to make the video flow smoothly. The *production phase* of the video montage involves the taping of scenes in sequence without being concerned with the audio, which will be added by the use of *audio dubbing*. The *postproduction phase* of video montage involves writing the script to accompany the sequence of scenes and adding a musical background if desired. Students and parents can be actively involved in the planning and taping of a video montage once the teacher is comfortable with the technique. Montage is especially appropriate for beginning videographers since it requires minimal preproduction planning and can be taped in sequence, eliminating the need for editing equipment.

REFERENCES

Caine, R. N. & Caine, G. (1991). *Making connections: Teaching and the human brain*. Alexandria, VA: Association for Supervision and Curriculum Development.

Gardner, H. (1993). *Multiple intelligences: The theory in practice.* New York: Basic Books.

Graves, D. H. (1995). A tour of Segovia School in the year 2005. *Language Arts, 72,* 12–18.

Hepler, S. (1991). Talking our way to literacy in the classroom community. *The New Advocate, 4,* 179–191.

Nourie, B. L. (1990). Camcorders and classrooms. *The Clearing House, 63,* 363–365.

Staab, C. (1991). Talk in whole-language classrooms. In V. Froese (Ed.), *Whole language practice and theory* (pp. 17–49). Needham Heights, MA: Allyn & Bacon.

SUGGESTED READINGS

Baraloto, R. A., & Silvious, S. (1991). 1 + 1 + 30 = Instructional success. *School Library Media Activities Monthly, 7* (1), 36–38.

Baraloto, R. A., & Silvious, S. (1992). VCR: A new emphasis on the "C" in the classroom curriculum. *School Library Media Activities Monthly, 7* (8), 37–39.

Beasley, A. (1993). *Looking Great with Video.* Worthington, OH: Linwood Publishing.

Brown, K. (1993). Video production in the classroom, creating success for students and schools. *Tech Trends 38* (3), 32–35.

Carucio, S. (1991 March/April). Facilitating a student-produced video. *Media Methods.* 26–27, 54–55.

Forgatch, M. S. & Ransey, E. (1994). Boosting homework: A video tape link between families and schools. *School Psychology Review, 23* (3), 472–484.

Reese, P. (1991). Words of wisdom for a good video production. *Media and Methods, 27* (4), 54.

Tibbs, P. (1989). Video creation for junior high language arts. *Journal of Reading 32* (6), 558–559.

Camcorder Applications in the Language Arts

Inspiration and Instruction

Mrs. Miller stands at the door of her classroom as the children file in the morning after Back-to-School Night. "Mrs. Miller, Mrs. Miller," bubbles Danny, "My mom said she saw me reading the book I wrote on the video last night!"

"My dad said he didn't know school was so different now," added Carol. "He was really excited about the science experiments we were doing in the video. He said he didn't get to do real experiments 'til he was in high school!"

"My mom said she really liked the part where we explained all the steps in the writing process," said José. "She was worried about my spelling until she saw the video. Now she thinks the way we're learning to write is the way real authors write. I told her we ARE real authors!"

Mrs. Miller smiles and says, "Well, we better get to work this morning. I want to make some more videos to show your parents all the great work you're doing. Conferences are coming up in just a month!"

At the middle school down the road, students are busily practicing questions they will ask Mrs. Tenaga, their language arts teacher who has just published a book. The students are excited that they know a "real author," and they want to find out all about her experiences as an author and how she got her ideas. The video club has set up the camcorder and tripod, and the students have written a partial script to introduce Mrs. Tenaga, and then individual students will ask her a series of questions. Since their teacher has been gone for a week promoting her book, the substitute teacher has assisted the students in preparing for this grand welcome. As Mrs. Tenaga enters the classroom, one of the students leads her to the decorated "Author's Chair," another introduces the video, and the production begins.

Videotaping group interactions provides concrete examples for student reflections and parent conferences.

CHAPTER OBJECTIVES

As Mrs. Miller discovered, video productions can be used to demonstrate how schools are changing and how children are learning. Mrs. Tenaga experienced firsthand the thrill of being interviewed on camera. In this chapter, you will learn about the use of video in the language arts. By reading this chapter and completing the video practice activity, you will learn

1. Ways to use the preproduction strategies of storyboarding and script writing to make effective classroom videos.
2. Ways to use video to enrich instruction in the language arts.
3. Ways to use video to motivate students to become more engaged in language arts instruction.
4. Ways to use video to document and celebrate students' progress in reading, writing, speaking, and listening.
5. Ways to use video to help parents understand the innovative teaching strategies now being used in schools and how to support their children's learning.

USING SCRIPT WRITING AND STORYBOARDING TO MAKE EFFECTIVE CLASSROOM VIDEOS

When planning to present new information to students, it is often challenging to bring their experiences to mind and build on those experiences so that the new information becomes related to the more familiar. One way to do this is to create a video presentation that starts with the known and builds to new concepts and connections. Writing a script and then taping video to illustrate it is an effective way of helping students to understand new concepts. Older students can research and write scripts for videos as well. Before the script is written, you need to ask four questions (Beasley, 1995):

1. What are you trying to communicate?
2. Who will be the audience?
3. What are the objectives for the video?
4. How will you tell the story?

Answering these questions is important because the answers help determine the approach you take to the video. If the script does not seem to be working, go back to these questions and see if you have wandered from the original intent of the video. Writing scripts takes practice, and students need to be taught some techniques. Help them to realize the power of the video and encourage them to "show" rather than tell all the details. Encourage students to try out their dialogue on other students to see if it is understandable and believable.

Not all videos require full scripts. When a story is being told with visual images, the script should be very complete so that the images (videotape) can be chosen to illustrate the message. In the case of interviews, sports events, or other video in which the words will be spontaneous, use a partial script. The introductory remarks are scripted and then the partial script simply notes that the person being interviewed will speak and an approximate time allowed. If any special camera angles or effects are needed, these are noted on the script. At the end of the partial script, the closing remarks are scripted (Beasley, 1995).

To plan the sequence of videotaping for a project, a script must be written and storyboards prepared so that each shot is carefully orchestrated. Preparing a storyboard includes planning shot size, shot length, camera movement, and text that will accompany the shot. Various formats are used for preparing storyboards but it is important to prepare each shot in sequence so you get a feel for the relationship of the shots and do not tell the whole story in medium close up. Figure 2.1 shows a storyboard page ready to be completed.

Note that the abbreviations for the shot sizes and camera movements are spelled out at the bottom of Figure 2.1. The shot number is placed in the box at the upper left of each storyboard scene. When the shot changes, you go to the next number. If you are simply zooming or panning within the same scene, you use the same shot number and add a letter; shot 1 might be a medium close-up of the teacher and shot 1A might be a zoom in to a close-up of the same scene. If the next shot moves to a classroom scene, it is numbered shot 2. The triangle on the left side of the box is used to note whether the shot is a take (T), zoom (Z), or pan (P), or other camera movement. Within the drawing section of the storyboard square, a rough sketch of the scene is made, showing the shot size and how much of the scene is desired. The length of the scene, in seconds, is noted under the triangle. The direction line is used to write exact directions to the camera person, for example, if scene 1 was a medium shot and scene 1A is to be a zoom to medium close-up, the directions line says, "Slow zoom to MCU."

The text line shows what is being said during this scene. If the text is to be recorded on camera, the line starts with (OC) so the cameraperson knows the audio is shot along with the video. If the text is to be added as a voice over, the text line starts with (VO). See Figure 2.2 for samples of storyboard scenes including all of these directions.

The remainder of this chapter introduces you to video applications in teaching language arts, as well as motivating and assessing students in the language arts with the use of video projects. As a part of these projects, you will be practicing script writing and storyboarding. Remember that the storyboard artwork

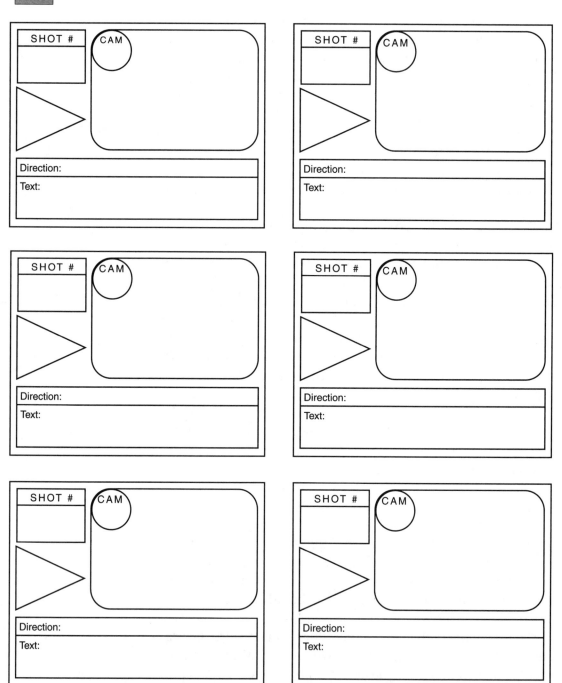

WS = wide shot   MX = med shot   MCU = med close-up   CU = close-up   ECU = extreme close-up
P = pan   T = take   Z = zoom   TT = tilt   D = dolly   A = arc   TR = truck   CC = camcor

F I G U R E   *Sample Storyboard Sequence*

2.2

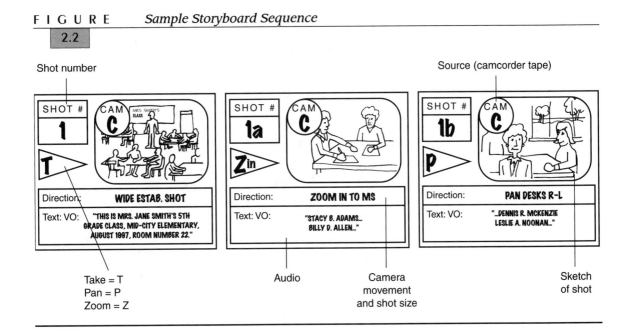

Shot number

Source (camcorder tape)

Take = T
Pan = P
Zoom = Z

Audio

Camera
movement
and shot size

Sketch
of shot

can be done with stick figures, the idea is to plan your shots and sequences, not to create a masterpiece of art.

USING VIDEO TO ENRICH LANGUAGE ARTS INSTRUCTION

In almost every phase of learning, some concepts seem difficult for students to grasp. Use of visuals to add context and illustrations to teaching has long been an accepted way of making instruction more understandable (Hyerle, 1996; Krashen, 1991; Bennett, 1990). Video is a very powerful teaching tool because it adds not only the visual but also action, language, and expression. The use of video allows the teacher to give real-life examples without leaving the classroom and to involve students in role-play and simulation activities with the added advantage of letting them actually view their performances. Story simulation activities represent one method of teaching students about characterization, character motivation, use of dialogue and description, and numerous other concepts that are sometimes difficult for them to comprehend.

Instruction in Vocabulary and Description

To interest students in using words to paint pictures, short video clips of people acting out scenes is an effective use of video to begin to build vocabulary and practice description. Prepare a videotape in which a student enters the room, head down, feet shuffling, body language implying defeat. Show the video clip and ask students to jot down words that describe what they have seen.

As a group, brainstorm words that can be used to describe movement, emotions, facial expressions, and body language, and list them on a large chart. Show the video clip again and give the students a few minutes to write a short paragraph describing the student's actions and adding some description of why the person is feeling the way she does. Give the students a chance to share their paragraphs and compare and contrast their ideas. Let the students work in groups of two or three to write a scenario and then let the groups videotape their scenes, with one person from the group reading the descriptive paragraph while the others act out the scene.

View the videotapes as a class and discuss the new vocabulary learned and nuances of meaning and then critique the videos and their effectiveness in demonstrating the meaning of the written descriptions.

Other video teaching possibilities will appear once you begin to think of the video camera as a teaching medium. Every time a student has difficulty understanding a concept or strategy, think of ways to illustrate it visually; often the video camera can be helpful.

Young children and second language learners benefit from having visuals to support their vocabulary development. Showing a video that illustrates a process in advance can help them to understand what is expected of them and lower their anxiety level. Illustrating new vocabulary with video is often easier and less expensive than taking still pictures and having the film developed. It is also much more graphic and is more closely related to their experiences. Introducing vocabulary with video shots of things familiar to the students is more helpful than using generic pictures of the same words. Use of the video also provides opportunities for the student to view a tape multiple times, which is often necessary in building language skills.

For older students, preparing music videos to demonstrate the meaning of new vocabulary is very motivating. Vocabulary Enterprises Co. has produced a series of music videos and raps that demonstrate the meaning of advanced vocabulary (see Appendix B, Teacher Resources, for more information). Middle and high school students can write and perform similar raps or role-plays demonstrating their understanding of new vocabulary. Videotaping their performances allows the teacher to use the videos in multiple classes, giving more students a chance to appreciate the efforts of their peers as well as learning the meanings of new words.

Videotaping students' presentations serves two important purposes. The students get to view and celebrate their accomplishments, and the teacher has a positive example to use as a sample for future classes.

Poetry and Visual Imaging

Teaching poetry as a form of painting pictures with words becomes more meaningful if students are given the opportunity to use video to interpret the poems. Listening to poetry and matching visual images with those brought to mind with the words is a custom-made activity for a video project. The students can use pictures found in books, art prints, or staged scenes to demonstrate the meaning of poetry. The simplicity of this type of video assignment makes it a joy for students and teachers alike. The students use the video camera to capture a series of visual images related to the images brought forth in the poem being illustrated. No audio is necessary. The audio is supplied by the reading of the poem as the video is viewed. Some students prefer to add a musical accompaniment along with the reading of the poem to help set the mood.

Story Simulations

Using videotape to document students' dramatic productions of literature is an innovative way to integrate all four language modes: reading, writing, speaking, and listening. First the literature must be read, then a script is prepared for the video, and parts are selected. A variety of roles is included in making such a production. Some students can be involved in preparing "video prompters" for the actors and actresses. Others can be involved in securing props and preparing backdrops. Others can actually serve as camerapersons. As older students become involved in this sort of production, they can do the preproduction planning and even prepare the shooting sequence and storyboards with visuals showing the content of each shot in the sequence.

With younger students, a less structured approach for story simulation that integrates all four language modes might involve orally reading the first chapter of a book to focus on how authors introduce characters and setting at the beginning of a book. The lesson plan and shooting sequence for this type of lesson might look like the following.

CHARLOTTE'S WEB Story Simulation

OBJECTIVE
After reading the first chapter of CHARLOTTE'S WEB, the students will be able to identify the main characters, give characteristics of each character, and write a letter from the characters' points of view.

VIDEO OBJECTIVE
The sequence of this video will document the way that the students recognized the character development in the book, identified the way that E. B. White helped the reader to become acquainted with the characters, acted out the roles of the main characters, and wrote a letter to Grandma Arable from the characters' points of view.

MATERIALS NEEDED
Copies of CHARLOTTE'S WEB, chalkboard and chalk, pretend or real microphone, pig puppet, writing paper and pencils, wig, bonnet or granny glasses for Grandma Arable, camcorder and videotape.

MOTIVATION
"I want you to listen to the first chapter of this book and see how many characters are introduced. Listen for things that help you get to know each character."

PROCEDURES:
1. Read the first chapter of CHARLOTTE'S WEB with expression.
2. After reading the chapter, ask the children to name the characters introduced in the chapter.

3. Write the names of the characters on the chalkboard as the children name them. Be sure to include Wilbur.
4. Ask the children to tell you what they know about each character just from hearing this first chapter. List the characteristics they identify under each character's name. Ask the children HOW they knew each of the things named. Encourage them to see that the author helped the reader to get to know the characters by using dialogue and description.
5. Ask for a volunteer to play each of the characters: Mr. Arable, Mrs. Arable, Fern, Avery, and Wilbur. Have the five volunteers come to the front of the room. Give the Wilbur puppet to the Wilbur character.
6. Explain that a news reporter from the local TV station has come to the Arable farm to interview the family about "the happenings" on the farm that morning. Play the part of the news reporter and ask each character to explain what happened. Sample questions might include the following:

   To Fern—How did you talk your dad into saving the pig's life?

   To Avery—Do you think it's fair that Fern got to keep the pig?

   To Mr. Arable—Why did you allow Fern to talk you into saving the runt piglet?

   To Mrs. Arable—Do you think Fern will be able to care for the pig all by herself?

   To Wilbur—What do you think about all the fuss made about you this morning?

7. After the TV interviews, divide the class into five groups with one of the character volunteers in each group. Instruct the groups to write a letter to Grandma Arable telling her about the morning's events from their character's point of view. Elicit a brief example of what each character might have to say in the letter. Emphasize that although only one person need actually write the letter, all members of the group need to help decide what to say. Emphasize that the letter must be written FROM the character to Grandma Arable and that the group should focus on what its character might say about the morning's events.
8. Circulate among the groups to provide help and encouragement.
9. Collect the letters, put on Grandma Arable's costume (wig or granny glasses), and read the letters aloud as if Grandma Arable were reading them.

CLOSURE
Briefly discuss what the children learned about developing characters and point of view. Ask the students to point out things written in the

letters that indicated that they were written from different points of view. The following is an example of one child's letter.

Dear Granny Arable,

I'm your new grand pig, Wilbur. Fern saved me from being axed to death today. Fern thinks I'm beautiful. She feeds me with a bottle. Please come visit. I vhant to meet you.

Love

wilber

Shooting Sequence for CHARLOTTE'S WEB STORY Simulation

Scene 1	Sign "Charlotte's Web."
Scene 2	Clip of teacher reading the first chapter of the book.
Audio	"Mr. Wynn read the first chapter of CHARLOTTE'S WEB aloud to the class."
Scene 3	Clip of teacher writing the characters and characteristics of each on the board. Zoom in to show the list of characters and their traits on the chalkboard.
Audio	"After the first chapter of the book was read, the children listed the characters who were introduced and what they learned about each character."
Scene 4	Clip of sign that says "Later that day."
Audio	"Now the students will play the parts of the Arable family as a news reporter interviews them about the morning's events."
Scene 5	Clip of the news interviews.
Scene 6	Wide shot of the class working in five groups.

Audio	"The class is now divided into five groups, one for each of the characters introduced."
Scene 7	Clips of each of the groups writing its letter.
Audio	"Each group is writing a letter to Grandma Arable describing the morning's events from its character's point of view."
Scene 8	Sign, "Later at Grandma Arable's House."
Scene 9	Grandma Arable reading her mail.
Scenes 10, 11, 12	Series of three signs: "The End," "The Characters," and "The Class."

Note that this video sequence can be taped without the use of a storyboard. Addition of the storyboard makes the videotaping easier, however, since each scene, camera shot, and camera movement are carefully planned. The CHARLOTTE'S WEB storyboard might look like the one in Figure 2.3.

Story simulations can be used at almost every level. Using the video to reenact literature gives students an opportunity to write scripts from the dialogue included in the literary piece, analyze the form of language, and make choices about actions or dialogue that must be added to make the story line clear. The study of great writers is enhanced through the use of video simulations. These can be done in the form of reader's theater without elaborate props and endless rehearsal. The importance of voice, expression, and gesture becomes very clear in the reader's theater format. The production is performed with scripts and very minimal props. Viewing the video production then sparks discussion of expression and motivation and allows the students to think more deeply about the play and the characterizations given by their peers. Because of the minimal time spent rehearsing, the play can be redone with different actors so that everyone gets an opportunity to add his personal interpretations.

With older students, selected scenes from a piece of literature can be chosen, a script written, and a storyboard drawn. Some students can serve as production engineers while others act the parts. Several groups can reenact the same scene adding unique characterizations. Once the class views the videos, the students can decide which reenactment most closely resembles their personal image of how the scene was intended to be played.

SHOT # **1**

F

Direction: **FADE IN FROM BLACK**

Text: VO: **MR. WYNN READS THE FIRST CHAPTER OF CHARLOTTE'S WEB ALOUD TO THE CLASS.**

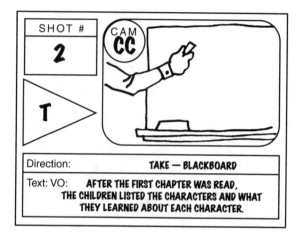

SHOT # **2**

T

Direction: **TAKE — BLACKBOARD**

Text: VO: **AFTER THE FIRST CHAPTER WAS READ, THE CHILDREN LISTED THE CHARACTERS AND WHAT THEY LEARNED ABOUT EACH CHARACTER.**

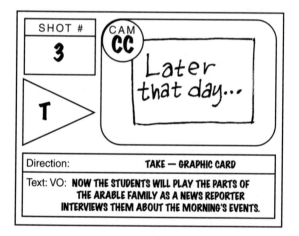

SHOT # **3**

T

Direction: **TAKE — GRAPHIC CARD**

Text: VO: **NOW THE STUDENTS WILL PLAY THE PARTS OF THE ARABLE FAMILY AS A NEWS REPORTER INTERVIEWS THEM ABOUT THE MORNING'S EVENTS.**

SHOT # **4**

T

Direction: **REPORTER INTERVIEWS**

Text: OC:

SHOT # **5**

T

Direction: **TAKE — GROUPS WORKING**

Text: VO: **THE CLASS IS NOW DIVIDED INTO FIVE GROUPS. ONE FOR EACH OF THE CHARACTERS INTRODUCED.**

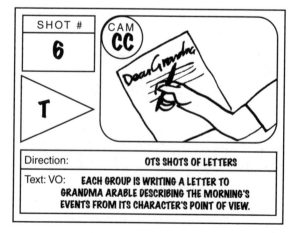

SHOT # **6**

T

Direction: **OTS SHOTS OF LETTERS**

Text: VO: **EACH GROUP IS WRITING A LETTER TO GRANDMA ARABLE DESCRIBING THE MORNING'S EVENTS FROM ITS CHARACTER'S POINT OF VIEW.**

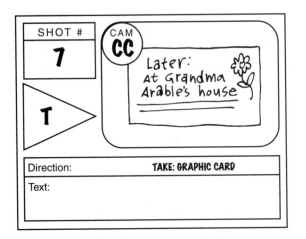

SHOT # **7**

CAM **CC**

Later: At Grandma Arable's house

Direction: **TAKE: GRAPHIC CARD**

Text:

SHOT # **8**

CAM

Direction: **TAKE: GRANDMA ARABLE**

Text: OC:

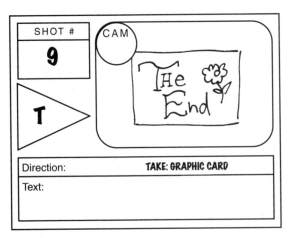

SHOT # **9**

CAM

The End

Direction: **TAKE: GRAPHIC CARD**

Text:

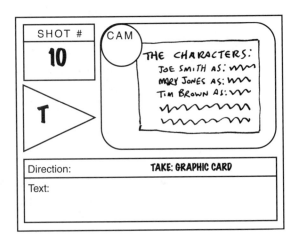

SHOT # **10**

CAM

THE CHARACTERS:
JOE SMITH AS:
MARY JONES AS:
TIM BROWN AS:

Direction: **TAKE: GRAPHIC CARD**

Text:

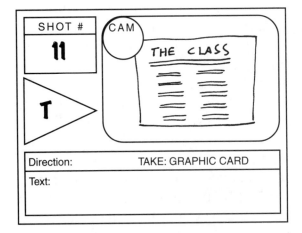

SHOT # **11**

CAM

THE CLASS

Direction: TAKE: GRAPHIC CARD

Text:

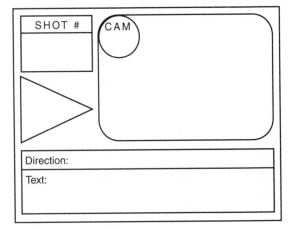

SHOT #

CAM

Direction:

Text:

The Use of Video in Teaching Group Interaction Skills

Although much has been said about the use of collaborative groups and interactive approaches in the schools, it is often difficult for teachers to use them in classrooms because of classroom management problems. For collaborative groups to be used effectively, students must understand their roles and the rules of verbal interaction (Manning & Lucking, 1993). Video can be used to help students to understand how these group interaction skills work. When setting up groups for literature discussion, for example, videotaping can be used as a "process observer."

Students in Bruce Thele's fifth grade class, were reading biographies of people instrumental in the American Revolutionary War. As he discusses the students' reading with them in literature groups, Mr. Thele asks the students to listen carefully to each other as they discuss the book they are reading. He says, "As you give your thoughts about the book, I want to see that you have been listening to the others who have been sharing. Refer to something the other person said. You can agree or disagree or add another thought, but make it clear that you have been listening to each other." The video camera is set up on a tripod near the literature discussion group and records the interactions as the students discuss their reading.

After the group discussion, Mr. Thele plays the tape back, and the students note the interactions. They point out the students who are obviously listening, as well as those who are too anxious to talk and didn't refer back to anything said by the others. Some of the students note personal attributes, both negative and positive. One boy says, "I talk too much. I don't give anyone else a chance." A girl notes, "I talk so softly no one can hear me." Mr. Thele helps the students to set personal goals for themselves for the next literature discussion group and repeats the process a few days later. The students are learning how to interact in groups.

When groups are formed for any reason—writing scripts or staging simulations, for example— the use of the video camera helps the students to reflect on their own participation. Often students are unaware of the way in which they interact in groups. Reflecting on the interactions after the group has met

Keeping a camcorder set up in the classroom at all times enables you to use it more effectively. It becomes just a piece of furniture and the students tend to ignore it. Their videotaped classroom interactions become much more natural.

and hearing the comments of their peers is often a learning experience. It is important for the teacher to set the tone for the activity and to keep the reflection process positive. The rules for discussion are to (1) give positive feedback first, (2) make suggestions as helpful as possible, and (3) evaluate yourself and set goals for next time.

Once videos are created, they should be used in ways that do the following:

- Document learning.
- Provide motivation for students.
- Inform teachers and parents about students' interests and strengths to facilitate future learning.
- Provide students with ideas on which to build.

Viewing the *Charlotte's Web* video described earlier in which students explored E. B. White's approach to character development enables students to improve their character development in writing. It may also give students ideas about additional video productions that can be created revolving around other literature and writers. It may help parents understand the ways in which their children interact in classroom settings and the ways that new approaches and technology are being used in classrooms today.

VIDEOTAPING AS MOTIVATION IN LANGUAGE ARTS

Video Book Reports

Motivating uninspired readers and writers can be facilitated with the use of video. Most students enjoy seeing themselves on television. Giving them the chance to write and videotape a commercial for a favorite book helps motivate them both to read (a necessity before the commercial can be made) and to write the commercial. Performing the commercial in front of the video camera gives students a chance to practice reading skills as well as to find innovative ways to interest other potential readers in the book being advertised.

Sometimes a student is not inspired to write a book report in the traditional manner. A video book commercial is a way to allow the student to come up with a more interesting way to present the book and convince others to read it. One inspired media teacher kept track of the number of requests for individual books each week after the book commercials were made available in the school media center. She then presented a "commercial award" to the video presenter whose book was the most frequently requested during the week.

Now that research on multiple intelligences is available (Gardner, 1993), we know that allowing students to document their learning in the mode of their stronger intelligence is helpful in motivating increased participation in the classroom. A child who has strengths in visual intelligence might enjoy creating a poster or scenery setting to be used in the delivery of the book commercial. A student who has strong kinesthetic intelligence might enjoy creating a mime presentation or a dance related to the book read. This presentation then can become a part of the book commercial. Students with interpersonal intelligence might want to work with another student or students to recreate some of the scenes from the book as a part of the commercial. Students with intrapersonal intelligence as a strength might enjoy creating a "paper bag book report" in which they put items in a paper bag that remind them of certain scenes or features in the book. They can then pull things out of the bag and give hints as to why the items made them think of the book. This type of book report is often very interesting to other students because the items used for the report add mystery to it almost compelling them to read the book to find out how all the items are connected to the text.

Allowing the students to be creative in the format of the book commercial is motivational, it builds on the strengths and interests of the individual, and videotaping the presentations allows you to document these strengths and interests and use them as part of a conference with parents.

Celebrating Story Versions

As students begin to read multiple versions of the same story, video can be used as they act out the various versions, write new versions, and contrast and compare them. A professional videotape of the movie *West Side Story* could be used to introduce older students to the study of *Romeo and Juliet*. Taking this one step further, the students could write additional versions of the same story line, setting it in various times in history. Costuming and acting of the versions could be coordinated with historical studies.

Creating Venn diagrams of two versions of the same story could be used as a planning activity for rewriting the story in a third version. Figure 2.4 is an example of a Venn diagram used to compare versions of a story.

Videotaping the process the students go through as they read, analyze, and plan versions of the story shows their comprehension of the plot, setting, and historical and social concerns of the various times in history.

Older students also enjoy planning the videotaping process. They can often improve upon their sense of story structure and characterization through the planning they do in making a videotape production. Having to show a character's emotional reactions in a video sequence is often helpful to students' reading expression and their writing of dialogue and description.

F I G U R E   *Venn Diagram showing story comparisons*
2.4

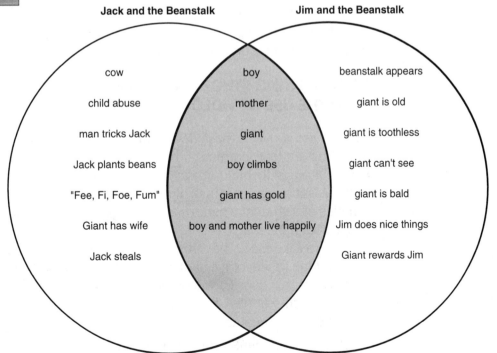

Jack and the Beanstalk   **Jim and the Beanstalk**

Jack and the Beanstalk	(shared)	Jim and the Beanstalk
cow	boy	beanstalk appears
child abuse	mother	giant is old
man tricks Jack	giant	giant is toothless
Jack plants beans	boy climbs	giant can't see
"Fee, Fi, Foe, Fum"	giant has gold	giant is bald
Giant has wife	boy and mother live happily	Jim does nice things
Jack steals		Giant rewards Jim

Documenting Oral Presentations

Oral presentations are often used as culminating activities in various subjects throughout the curriculum. The presentation skills necessary for students to make effective oral presentations are often not given much attention. Often students dread standing in front of the class, and their presentations do not always improve over time because they are not given a chance to view and critique themselves. Videotaping oral presentations and then allowing the presenter to view and critique her own presentation is one way to help the student set goals for herself, identify areas to improve in the future, and to understand the purpose of the use of visuals and gestures in public speaking. Using a demonstration tape to show some of the important points to remember in making an oral presentation helps the students to plan effective visuals and incorporate gestures and facial expression in their presentations. Just knowing ahead of time that their presentation will be videotaped is often a strong motivation for students to do extra planning and to practice more. In the beginning, the viewing and critiquing should be a private matter. Allowing the student to view the tape privately and list areas of strengths and goals for improvement before sharing the tape with the teacher or parents is an effective way to begin to encourage reflection and self-evaluation.

DOCUMENTING STUDENT LEARNING WITH THE USE OF VIDEO

Everywhere you look these days, you see information about documenting student learning through portfolios. One of the most powerful ways to build portfolios is through the use of video. Nothing is more graphic than a parent and teacher viewing actual samples of a student's performance and being able to back up in time through the magic of video to view a previous performance. For this to take place, however, a teacher must plan ahead and find the time to videotape student performance periodically. One way to do this is to use a videotaping schedule to tape one or two students each day. The following are suggestions for finding the time to do this videotaping:

1. Have one student a day come in a few minutes early to be videotaped.

2. Ask older students or "video helpers" to do the actual videotaping. Some schools have a video club whose helpers are trained to provide this service.
3. Have a few students stay after school one afternoon a week on a rotating basis to make "student progress videos."
4. Tape group interactions as activities are taking place during the class day.

What Should Be Taped?

Your language arts objectives will determine the types of videos you will want to make. Video can be used to document students' individual growth, demonstrate strategies in reading and writing, allow students to dramatize their writing and reading, motivate readers and writers, help parents to understand the curriculum and many other things. As you become more familiar with the videotaping process other applications will emerge—both from the teachers and the students.

A video portfolio can be made to include a variety of samples of a child's progress. In language arts, the video samples should document the important strategies and skills being learned. The students themselves can often help to plan the samples they would like to include on their videotape, but samples of the basics such as reading fluency and comprehension and writing progress should be documented periodically throughout the year. This takes planning and consistency.

The form of the student progress videotape varies depending upon what is being documented. For example, to document a student's growth in oral reading fluency, the student should be videotaped on a regular schedule so that ongoing progress (or lack of it) is evident. This involves maintaining a schedule of reading sample video over the course of the year so that each child is videotaped periodically, at regular intervals. A cyclical shooting schedule is helpful to keep this schedule organized. Figure 2.5 shows a way to organize and keep track of the videotaping schedule.

Videotaping two students a day allows you to cycle through a class of 30 students in three weeks. The two students could come in early or stay late for a few minutes. This example allows videotaping of individual reading samples at six-week intervals throughout the school year.

F I G U R E

2.5

*Cycle
Shooting
Schedule*

Student Names	Dates of Individual Reading Samples (Circle when complete)					
Danny	9/1	10/16	12/2	1/15	3/5	5/14
Anthony	9/1	10/16	12/2	1/15	3/5	5/14
Xong	9/2	10/17	12/3	1/16	3/6	5/15
Dua	9/2	10/17	12/3	1/16	3/6	5/15
Evan	9/3	10/18	12/4	1/17	3/7	5/16
Nancy	9/4	10/19	12/5	1/18	3/8	5/17
Grace	9/4	10/19	12/5	1/18	3/8	5/17
Toni	9/5	10/20	12/6	1/19	3/9	5/18
Irvin	9/5	10/20	12/6	1/19	3/9	5/18

If a student's use of the writing process is being documented, video clips of the student doing prewriting activities, sharing drafts of a work in progress with other students, revising the draft based on the feedback of peers, editing with peers, and presenting a final piece of work in published form should all be a part of the student's writing portfolio. Although these steps can be documented using work samples and still photos, it is easy to see how much more vivid the video samples would be. In most cases, documenting the growth of individual students should be done on individual tapes for each student. The students themselves can help to maintain the schedule for documenting the writing process stages. A classroom chart on which the students sign up for videotaping as they progress through the writing process is helpful to the organization of this process. Figure 2.6 shows an example of such a chart for videotaping. Each child signs up on it as he enters new stages of the writing process. The child gets the individual tape out and has it ready as the videographer comes around the

F I G U R E

2.6

Writing Process Sign-up Chart

Sign up to be videotaped as you begin each stage of the writing process.

Prewriting	Drafting	Conferring	Revising	Editing	Publishing	Celebrating

classroom taping individuals as they plan, write, confer, revise, edit, publish, and present the finished work (celebrate).

A "history of a writing project" is a valuable piece of the video portfolio. Clips made at each stage of the process (prewriting, drafting, conferring, revising, editing, and publishing) allow the teacher to evaluate the way the student is using the process, and identify places where the student tends to get "stuck" and the resources that the student uses in supporting his/her writing. It is especially vital always to videotape the students as they celebrate the publication of a new book and add that book to the growing collection of student-published books in the classroom. Just the act of videotaping that celebration proves very motivational for many students.

This kind of documentation, along with writing samples and teacher and student evaluation of the samples, helps motivate the students to set goals for themselves and celebrate their own progress. This attention to individual growth and goal setting is often the spark that motivates young learners. In addition, parents appreciate having the opportunity to view this type of proof of a child's progress in school.

Preproduction Planning for Documenting Learning

Several elements are involved in planning for documentation of student learning. First, the students should understand what is being done and have an opportunity to prepare for their videotaping. They should be given a choice of materials to use in the videotaping. If the fluency of their oral reading is the focus of the taping, make a shooting plan that allows the viewer actually to follow along with the text being read. For very young children who are "telling" the story from illustrations rather than actually decoding text, it is vital that the viewer be able to see what the text actually says while the child's voice is heard "reading." For older students whose interpretation of the text involves more gestures, body language, and facial expression, these features need to be very visible on the tape. If you plan to tape clips, instead of the entire reading, you will have a chance to switch camera positions periodically. This all needs to be noted on the preproduction plan as shown in Figure 2.7. Figure 2.8 provides video tips for taping an individual reading sample.

Documenting the Writing Process

Many parents have questions about the way writing is being taught today. The process approach to writing may be an entirely new strategy to many. Using video to document the stages in the writing process, ways that writing is supported and shared in the classroom, and some of the newer techniques such as the use of invented (or temporary) spelling in drafts helps parents to become more supportive of these approaches. An introductory video showing how the classroom is organized for Reading/Writing

FIGURE

2.7

Preproduction Plan for Individual Reading Samples

Shot 1	Student holding the book, reading the title and author (medium close-up)
Audio	My name is _____. Today is _____. I will read _____ by _____.
Shot 2	Clip of student beginning to read book. (close-up)
Shot 3	Over-the-shoulder shot of text as student reads. (close-up)
Shot 4	Later in the book, over-the-shoulder shot of text as student reads. (close-up)
Shot 5	Later in the book. Front shot for expression. (medium close-up)
Shot 6	After the book is read. Child tells the favorite or most interesting part.

FIGURE

2.8

Video Tips for Individual Reading Sample

1. Frame the student carefully, allowing adequate head room in the shot. Make sure the background is not distracting.
2. Seat the student so you have enough room to move behind her for over-the-shoulder shots.
3. Practice the introductory statement before filming it. Make sure the student is speaking slowly and clearly.
4. Prepare the student ahead of time for the movements you will make with the camera. As you move around to shoot over the shoulder, encourage her to continue reading.
5. If the student becomes flustered, use your in-camera edit. Rewind the tape to a natural break (change of shot) and retape.

Workshop and the ways that students are empowered by making topic choices for their reading and writing is important in helping parents understand the process before they view examples of their own child's individual progress. This way, the parents understand the process before it becomes personal.

Having a video camera handy in the classroom during Reading/Writing Workshop is one very important way to validate the students' efforts in these areas. Showing the way the students have more control over the choice of topics and use of time in the classroom helps keep the students on task more and allows the teacher to show the parents how the process works. For the teacher to be able to document each of the steps in the writing process on tape takes careful planning.

Figure 2.9 shows how this might be accomplished in video.

FIGURE

2.9

Writing Process Video

	Video	Audio
	THE WRITING PROCESS (sign) :5	Today's students are learning to write using a process similar to one that real authors use.
	Close-up of a student drawing a picture, another student drawing a web, a third student making an outline. :06	Before the writing begins, the author plans the story and things that will be included. Sometimes this is done with a picture, a web, or an outline.
	Close-up of a student writing a story draft. :05	Once an idea is formed, the student writes a draft of the story. At this point, the important thing is ideas. Spelling, mechanics, and sequence are not important.
	Medium shot of a group of students reading their drafts and giving each other suggestions. :08	After the writer has a first draft written, he reads the draft to the teacher or a group of students.
	Continue the conference scene and listen to the students' comments as they give each other suggestions. :15	Listen to the students.
	Medium shot of a student returning to his seat, sitting down, and revising. :05	After the conference, the student goes back to his seat and revises his draft, incorporating the suggestions made by his teacher or peers if he likes the suggestions.
	Medium shot of another conference with the same student reading his new draft. :05	This drafting, conferring, and revising can be repeated several times if needed.
	Medium shot of two students editing, using a dictionary, and entering proof marks. :06	Once the ideas are in place, the student is ready to edit for spelling and punctuation.
	Close-up of the edited piece. :04	After the piece is student edited, the student decides how he wants to publish his book.
	Close-up of various publication choices (books, big books, display boards). :04	The book format is chosen and the student publishes his book.
	Close-up of the student making the book cover and inserting the pages into the book. :05	The students work hard to make their finished books look good.

2.9	Video	Audio
(continued)	Medium shot of the student sitting in the author's chair and reading his book aloud. :06	The book is read aloud to the class as the student sits in the author's chair and the book is added to the class library.
	Medium pan of students holding published books with big smiles on their faces. :05	The students feel like real authors!
	Medium shot of students reading each others' published books. :04	They get lots of reading practice reading each other's published books.
	Total time 1:23	

Video Uses with Emergent Readers and Writers

As young children are emerging as readers and writers, their progress can be documented on video. The following are some suggestions for settings for videotaping:

1. Provide small props or costumes for the children to reenact stories they have heard. Videotape these unrehearsed productions periodically. Using these tapes in parent conferences allows the teacher to help parents to understand the importance of rereading familiar books and providing play props for children to retell favorite stories as well as the motivation of play as it relates to story reading and retelling.

2. Videotaping children in the classroom as they are given free-choice activities allows the teacher to become more aware of the choices a child makes and allows parents to see their children in action in the classroom, in many cases a very different context than the home setting.

3. Videotaping children as they experiment with writing and drawing allows the teacher to evaluate the progress each child is making in representing ideas in abstract ways. Observing the approach a child makes to the task of writing, the way he holds the pencil or crayon, any oral language the child uses as she writes or draws, and the stages of representation (from random scribbling all the way to actual sound/symbol

relationships) help the teacher to plan appropriate curricular activities for the children in the classroom.

4. Periodic videotaping of children sharing a favorite story-book can be scheduled on a regular basis, as described in the section on taping reading records.

USING VIDEO IN PARENT CONFERENCES

Using video in parent conferences allows the teacher to visu-ally demonstrate the student's growth, but it requires some planning. The video clips to be shown to the parents should be preselected and the videotapes cued to the exact point to be shown so that time is not wasted in searching for the clip. Older students can be involved in selecting the video clip they would like to share with their parents. In many cases, a parent-teacher-student conference is effective in creating more motivation and ownership on the part of the student. Video clips can be used to emphasize strengths as well as identify weaknesses and facilitate collaborative goal setting. Often parents can be helpful if they know exactly what they can do to help at home.

PRACTICE ACTIVITY

To practice writing a script and storyboarding, choose a piece of literature that you use with your students. Depending on the ages of the students, either write a script or involve them in writing it. Prepare a storyboard for the script and videotape the production. Show the video in your classroom and encourage the students to critique the script and video, looking at such things as the use of props, costumes, and dialogue and the way in which the characters were depicted. As you discuss the video, ask questions such as these:

- Did the characters talk the way you thought they would?
- Did the video show the scenes the way you pictured them when you read the book?

Encourage the students to talk about the images they had formed in their minds as they read the book and how these images changed as they watched the video.

EVALUATION OF THE VIDEO PRACTICE ACTIVITY

Reflect on the implementation of the video practice activity. Did you have any problems in the planning? What would you do differently next time? Make adjustments in your plans to reflect the things you learned in completing this assignment.

Evaluate the students' involvement. Were they fully involved in planning each step? How could they have been more involved? What did they learn from the exercise? Could the video be used for parent conferences? Goal setting? Motivation for future lessons?

VIDEO PROJECT

Now that you have had practice in writing a script and a storyboard, choose one example of a video project and implement it. The following are some suggestions for projects.

Partial Script Projects

• Videotape a grand conversation or collaborative group activity and give the students an opportunity to view their participation and set goals for themselves for future group interactions. Grand conversations are group discussions of a piece of literature; they enable the teacher to evaluate each student's understanding of the piece. Collaborative group activities might include one of the following

- A literature simulation.
- A puppet show or skit.
- A story rewrite and enactment.

• Invite a favorite author or illustrator to visit and involve the students in planning the questions they want to ask. Plan the order of the questioning and videotape the entire episode, scripting the introduction, sequence of questions, and the concluding remarks. View the videotape with the students and encourage them to evaluate their questioning techniques.

Full Script Projects

• Encourage the students to choose a scene from a favorite piece of literature and write a script for it. Videotape the performance and show the video to the class. Conduct a discussion focusing on the character interpretations in the video and the way the students pictured the scene as they read the book.

• Videotape book commercials written by the students. Encourage the students to write a script, draw a simple storyboard, dress in costume, or add some innovation before they are videotaped.

• Read two versions of the same book and encourage the students to compare them. Use the comparison of the stories to assist the students in writing a third version of the book. Videotape each step in the process and show the video to the class. Encourage the students to discuss the process they experienced and any new insights they gained about the books as they wrote a new version.

• Encourage the students to find new vocabulary that could be incorporated into a rap video. Allow them to write and perform short raps demonstrating the meaning of the vocabulary words they selected and videotape their performances. Encourage the students to use the vocabulary words in their speaking and writing and discuss their ability to use the vocabulary correctly after viewing the tapes.

Involve your students in planning and producing the video when it is appropriate. Remember the sequence of planning:

- List the objectives.
- Write a script.
- Plan a shooting sequence to illustrate the script.
- Create a storyboard for the shooting sequence.
- Shoot the scenes in sequence.

Implement the plan and use the video in a parent conference, parent meeting, or student evaluation session.

SUMMARY

This chapter introduced the preproduction strategies of scripting and storyboarding. Suggestions for implementing the use of video in the teaching, motivation, and assessment of the language arts include a number of techniques, such as these:

Story simulation.
Collaborative group activities.
Grand conversations or literature discussions.

Comparing and contrasting versions of a story.
Writing new versions of a story.
Video book reports.
Interviewing strategies.
Video portfolios.

The natural integration of language arts in any video project makes the use of these projects a strong motivation for student involvement and creativity. "The one requisite to incorporate video production into the curriculum is a teacher willing to try something different and, be assured, the students will supply the creativity" (Beasley, 1995).

CHILDREN'S BOOKS CITED

Briggs, R. (1970). *Jim and the Beanstalk*. New York: Coward-McCann.
Unknown (1965). *Jack and the Beanstalk*. New York: Scholastic.
White, E. B. (1952). *Charlotte's Web*. New York: Harper & Row.

REFERENCES

Beasley, A. (1995). Script writing. *School Library Media Activities Monthly, 11,* 35–38.
Bennett, C. (1990). Comprehensive multicultural education. *Theory and Practice,* 2nd ed. Boston, MA: Allyn & Bacon.
Gardner, H. (1993). *Multiple Intelligences: The Theory in Practice.* NY: Basic Books.
Hyerle, D. (1996). *Visual Tools for Constructing Knowledge.* Alexandria, VA: Association for Supervision and Curriculum Development.
Krashen, S. (1991). *Bilingual education: A focus on current research.* Washington, DC: National Clearinghouse for Bilingual Education.
Manning, M. L., and Lucking, R. (1993). Cooperative learning and multicultural classrooms. *The Clearing House 67,* 12–16.

SUGGESTED READINGS

Arnold, D. H., Lonigan, C. J., Whitehurst, G. J., and Epstein, J. N. (1994). Accelerating language development through picture book reading: Replication and extension to a videotape training format. *Journal of Education Psychology, 86* (2), 235–243.

Bledsoe, P. M. (1992). Performance and evaluation of communicative tasks: The video camera in the K-2 classroom. *Hispania, 75,* 15–21.

Botterbusch, H. R. (1991). Tune-in and turn-on! Videos in the Classroom. *Tech Trends, 36* (4), 22–24.

Heller, N. 1994. *Projects for New Technologies in Education Grades 6–9.* Englewood, CO: Teacher Ideas Press.

Sine, L., and Pensabene, S. (1991). Visual literacy: Using audiovisual presentation to make book reports come alive. *School Library Media Activities Monthly, 7* (4), 39–40+.

Weber, F. A. 1992. Video production and student storytelling in the elementary school library media center. *School Library Media Activities Monthly, 8* (6), 36–39.

Camcorder Applications in Science and Mathematics

Seeing Things Clearly

Mr. Jacobs stands in the back of his high school science classroom watching his students work with microscopes. Each pair of students is taking turns looking through the microscope on its lab table, talking to each other about what they are seeing.

Jan and Anthony are sharing a microscope in the back row of tables. Jan turns to Mr. Jacobs and says, "I never know if I'm looking at what you've been talking about or just a speck of dust. Microscopes are so frustrating."

Anthony is nodding his head. He shows Mr. Jacobs his drawing of the cells he sees through the microscope. "My drawing doesn't look anything like Jan's," he says. "Are we seeing the same thing, or is my drawing just bad?"

Mr. Jacob walks quickly to the front of the room and adjusts the camcorder he has set up on the eyepiece of his microscope. As the image from his microscope appears on the 29-inch screen of the television monitor, a low murmur of voices can be heard from the students, "Ooooh, that's what we're looking for!" says Jan. "Now I see it!"

After the students complete their lab work, Mr. Jacobs walks around the room looking at their lab journals. Several of the students admit to him that they had not even focused on the right part of their slide until he showed it on the television monitor. Mr. Jacobs says to the class members as they leave the room, "I'm sure glad I set up the camcorder today!"

In Ms. Bateman's fifth grade class, the students are discussing careers they would like to investigate. Many of the students in the class have parents who work in the space industry but seem to have only a general idea of what their parents do when they go to work.

"My dad is an engineer," says Sean.

"What kind of work does he do?" asks Ms. Bateman.

"He goes to a lot of meetings, and he draws plans. . ." Sean trails off. "I guess I need to talk to him. I don't know exactly what he does."

"That's a great idea," responds Ms. Bateman. "Maybe we need to think of questions we can ask our parents or other people we know who have interesting jobs. I particularly want you to ask questions about how they use science and math in their jobs."

The students spend the next 15 minutes brainstorming questions they will ask their parents that evening when Sean suddenly has an idea, "Ms. Bateman! Can we make a video about using math and science in different jobs?"

"That's a great idea! Sean," she replies. "Work on your interviews this evening and tomorrow we'll find out what you've learned and begin to plan our video. Then we'll be able to share our research with the other fifth grades."

Using the camcorder and microscope together allows the whole class to view more effectively.

CHAPTER OBJECTIVES

As Mr. Jacobs realizes, students sometimes need assistance in science and math observation either because the objects they are observing are very small or because the growth they are watching occurs very slowly. In Ms. Bateman's class, the students have become motivated by the prospect of using video to document their research and to integrate their studies in math and science by writing scripts, planning storyboards, and producing videos to share with others. In this chapter, you will learn about the use of video in enhancing observation as well as a variety of other strategies in these two areas. By reading this chapter and completing the video practice activity you will learn

1. To use video to enrich instruction in science and mathematics, including time-lapse and macro videotaping.
2. To use video to motivate students to become more actively involved in science and mathematics.
3. To use video to document and celebrate students' progress in scientific and mathematics processes and applications.
4. To help parents understand the innovative teaching strategies now being used in schools and ways to support their children's learning.

USING VIDEO TO TEACH SCIENCE AND MATH

As Mr. Jacobs demonstrated with the use of microscopes, students often benefit from visuals that help them focus on the task at hand. In learning scientific and mathematics processes, it is often necessary for the teacher to demonstrate with students observing. For whole class groups, the demonstrations are effective only if everyone can clearly see what is being demonstrated. In addition, video can demonstrate practical applications of science and math concepts. Students often don't make the connections between what they are learning in the classroom and what they need to understand to function in the "real world" (Mullis & Jenkins, 1988).

Using a camcorder and monitor in the classroom serves an important role in teaching demonstrations. Using the camcorder to show enlarged objects on the monitor makes them more visible to the entire class.

Video as Advance Organizer

Since we cannot assume that all students in the classroom have the same rich background of experiences, video can be used to provide some background knowledge as a new topic of study is introduced. It can also serve to give students a glimpse of the study to come as an advance organizer so that they have their minds in gear (Ausubel & Sullivan, 1970).

Sometimes commercial or premade videos serve the purpose of introducing a new topic of study, but they must be used with caution. To involve students as they watch a video, they must be prepared to watch for specific things or the answers to certain questions in the video. Figure 3.1 lists suggested planning and reviewing strategies for the use of video viewing in the classroom.

The KWL Chart

A simple strategy for using video to introduce a topic of study is the *KWL chart*. The teacher makes a three-sectioned chart on large paper and labels the sections Know—Want to Know—Learned. Before showing the video, the students brainstorm all they already know about the topic to be studied; they list these items under Know. At this point, the teacher accepts anything they *think* they know. Errors can be corrected after viewing the video or after further study of the topic. Next, students brainstorm things they would like to know about the topic and list

FIGURE

3.1

*Strategies
for Using
Video in the
Classroom*

1. The teacher must thoroughly preview the video and thoughtfully plan its use.
2. All students are given a clear instructional purpose for the use of the video. Active viewing is motivated by giving the students
   a. a preview of things to watch for.
   b. questions that the video will answer.
   c. some specific purpose for watching.
3. The teacher plans specific places in the video at which to stop, review, and discuss.
4. The teacher allots time for a thorough discussion of what was viewed.
5. As a follow-up, students are given an assignment in which they must expand the knowledge gained by viewing the video, contrast it to material they have read, or compare it to other experiences they have had.
6. Students who are absent are given a chance to view the video or review notes about it so that they have not missed the learning opportunity.
7. Video viewing is an active, learning experience, NOT something to replace teaching.

these items under Want to Know. Once these two steps are completed, the teacher instructs the students to watch the video, keeping the questions under Want to Know in mind. After the video is viewed, the information learned is added to the chart under Learned. If questions under Want to Know remain unanswered, the students are given the opportunity to add to the chart as the study progresses. The use of the KWL chart serves to relate the students' background knowledge to the topic of study and motivates them to watch the video and continue their study of the topic in more depth since they have identified areas of interest. Who knows? They may also learn the material required in the district's objectives.

Almost any science and math lesson that involves the teacher or a student demonstrating with manipulatives or equipment will be enhanced through the use of the camcorder directly connected to the television monitor. Use of the monitor allows everyone to view the demonstration more clearly. It also allows the demonstration to be videotaped for future use. Students who are absent that day have a chance to see what they missed. If it becomes evident that a review is necessary, the tape can be viewed again, and it can be used to show parents the types of activities that typically occur in the classroom. If the demonstration was done by students, copies of the tape can be included in their portfolios.

Video Tips

Use of the camcorder with a microscope requires several pieces of special equipment. The camcorder must be mounted on the eyepiece of the microscope using a mounting bracket specifically designed for this purpose. This bracket which can be purchased from microscope suppliers, comes in a variety of sizes to match the barrel of the microscope. To view what is being videotaped, two special direct connector cords must be connected from the camcorder to the television monitor. One cable connects the video output on the camcorder to the video input on the television monitor, and the second cable connects the audio output on the camcorder to the audio input on the television. (These connector cords are called RCA or BNC connection cords.)

In addition to the microscope mount, a low lux feature on the camcorder allows you to film with low light available, which is the situation with a microscope. If your camcorder does not have this low lux feature, you must use the most brightly lit microscope you can find. Your picture may be dark, but it should be visible.

A variety of camcorder, microscope combinations are available through scientific equipment suppliers, ranging between $1,000 and $30,000.

Videotaping Procedures for Using, Caring for, and Storing Materials

Procedures for using, caring for, and storing materials are important in science and math classrooms. Making a videotape demonstrating these procedures as they are explained at the beginning of the school year not only validates the importance of the procedures but also allows procedure reviews to be repeated periodically throughout the year as needed. One high school science teacher requires individual students to review the video when they violate procedures and routinely asks substitutes to view the video along with the students so that everyone involved knows what is expected.

Using the Camcorder in Nature Study

The use of the camcorder in studying nature allows the teacher to accomplish several very important objectives. Things that happen very slowly can be videotaped and then speeded up so that they can be more easily seen and understood. Planting a seed and observing its stages of growth viewed in minutes instead of weeks is only one example of this type of lesson. The formation and movement of clouds, the changing of shadows as the time of day changes, the building of a bird nest, and the life cycle of a frog or caterpillar can be viewed from a time-lapse videotape. Some camcorders come with a time-lapse feature, but a time-lapse can be shot manually simply by shooting a few seconds of tape periodically (see Figure 3.2).

Students can even be involved in an experiment to determine the best choice of time and scheduling for time-lapse video. By viewing several videotapes shot on different schedules, students can compare the results. This manual time-lapse video is not as professional as those obtained with a time-lapse feature built into the camera, but the students have the experience of trying different shooting durations and scheduling choices and comparing results, giving them more control over their experiments.

In addition to time-lapse video, close-up video is helpful in enlarging very small objects for close examination and study. A macro feature on the camcorder allows you to focus on small

FIGURE

*Tips for
Time-Lapse
Video*

Many higher-priced camcorders have electronic features such as interval recording—also know as time lapse—that on some Panasonic models, for example, allow automatic recording of 1 second, or about 30 frames, every minute up to 10 hours. This allows you to videotape events that occur slowly. A 10-minute video shows the growth or change that actually took 10 hours in real time. The operations manual for the camcorders with this feature includes specific instruction on setting up for interval recording. The easiest way to do time-lapse video is to invest in a camcorder that has a time-lapse feature. If this is not possible, the following manual time-lapse procedure can be followed:

1. Set up the camcorder on a tripod and focus on the image to be videotaped. Carefully mark the placement of the camera, tripod, and object to be videotaped with masking or gaffer's tape so the set-up may be duplicated at a later time and so any movement of the equipment is obvious.
2. Start this project on a Monday morning, if possible. This allows you to get as much action as possible during the week. If you know nothing will happen for a few days, set up the project on a Friday morning, videotape during the day, and then begin again on Monday.
3. Establish a schedule to be used, such as 5 to 10 seconds every hour, every two hours, and so on. Videotape on this schedule for as much of the day as possible.
4. Because you are not taping on a regular schedule as you would be with an automatic time-lapse camera, identify lapses in time with audio such as "three days later."
5. Resist the urge to videotape more frequently when action occurs. The action shows up with more time between shots.

Students can experiment with a variety of taping schedules to shoot the same object but changing tapes. It is important not to move the tripod or the object being taped, but one student could tape every hour for 10 seconds, another student could tape for 5 seconds every two hours, and so on. Students could then compare and contrast the tapes.

objects at a very close range. This enables the students to observe the objects more closely and the teacher to explain features that the students will need to recognize as they do their explorations. This is an extremely helpful feature and should be included if you have the chance to purchase a new camcorder.

Using the Camcorder in Mathematical Studies

Problem-Solving Strategies

Many of the newer math curricula involve students using manipulatives or graphics in solving math problems. These active-learning approaches emphasize the fact that there may be more than one way to solve a problem. In Mrs. McAleece's second grade class, the students have recently returned from a field trip to an aquarium and are continuing their study of sea creatures. Mrs. McAleece is posting a daily challenge question related to their study. Today's challenge question reads, "There are three hermit crabs. Each lives in five different shells during its lifetime. How many shells will the three use altogether?" As the second graders complete their morning assignments, they are encouraged to gather in groups of two or three to discuss the challenge question and decide on a solution. When each group decides on a solution, it must find a way, using manipulatives or visuals of some kind, to explain its solution to the class. Since the students know their presentation will be videotaped, they work hard on finding a way to present it to the class in an interesting way.

At the end of the day, three groups and one individual student are ready to make presentations. Mrs. McAleece sets up the camcorder and tripod and is ready to videotape their presentations. The first group is convinced that the answer to the question is 15. Its members have drawn a poster that shows three hermit crabs, each with 5 shells in graduated sizes, for a total of 15 shells. They explain their solution clearly, using a pointer to emphasize their drawings and the fact that the hermit crab changes shells only when it outgrows the old shell.

The second group has drawn a series of seven shells, each slightly larger than the last. Its solution involves each crab moving into the next larger shell as it is vacated so that the crabs are using the same shells and require only a total of seven shells. This group gets several questions about whether members think that the crabs would all be ready to change shells at the same time. They handle the questions well, stating that since the crabs all live in the same part of the ocean, they will probably be growing at about the same rate.

The third group shows a diagram of seven shells in a circle and explains that its crabs change shells at the same time and simply move across the circle to find a vacated shell, much like the playground game Squirrels in the Tree. They admit forgetting that the crabs need bigger shells when they move.

Adam has a unique solution of his own and presents a solo presentation, mainly because he couldn't convince his group that his solution was a good one. He presents a drawing of five shells. He tells a story of a hermit crab family that begins with one hermit crab, whom he calls Grandpa and says that Grandpa moves into a larger shell only when his son is born and takes the first, smaller shell when Grandpa moves into the second shell. Grandpa and son each move up a shell when another baby crab is born, so that Grandpa is now in shell 3, son in shell 2, and baby in shell 1. When they outgrow those shells, each moves up to a larger shell, now occupying shells 3, 4, and 5. When Grandpa dies, son and baby move into shells 4 and 5 and when son dies, baby moves into shell 5 so that only five shells are necessary. Adam's solution sets off a flurry of discussion, including how the babies can be born without a mother hermit crab, whether it is fair to "kill off the crabs" as a part of the solution. Mrs. McAleece pulls the discussion together by asking the students ways that they can resolve the problems. They decide that they must research how hermit crabs reproduce and how long they live before they know whether Adam's solution can be accepted. The students' questions are listed on the chalkboard, and a group of students is assigned to bring more information back to the group the next day. See Figure 3.3 for the children's solutions to the hermit crab problem.

Mrs. McAleece is pleased by the variety of solutions the students presented and by the care they took in preparing their

FIGURE
3.3

Children's Solution to the Hermit Crab Problem

Group One's Solution

Group Two's Solution

Group Three's Solution

Adam's Solution

presentations. She saves the videotape to show at parent meetings next week. She wants to show how much thought the students are putting into finding alternative solutions to math and science problems, ways they are beginning to use their research skills to explore problem solving more deeply, and ways their discussion and group interaction skills are progressing. She finds that using the camcorder to capture these group interactions in math and science class helps her to recognize the unique problem-solving approaches of individual students in her class.

Teaching Practical Applications in Math

Mr. Morales teaches middle school math. He is demonstrating the use of sampling and polls to determine the probable outcome of the upcoming national election. He divides his class into groups of four students and pours M&Ms into a huge bowl, saying, "Each of the M&Ms in this bowl represents a voter who will help elect the president of the United States. Red M&Ms will vote for candidate A, greens will vote for candidate B, oranges will vote for candidate C, and so on." Mr. Morales lists all the other colors of the M&Ms and their candidates on the chalkboard. He then has each of the groups come up to the bowl and dip a small cup full of M&Ms out of the bowl. The groups go back to their seats and spread their M&Ms out on the table. Mr. Morales goes from group to group, videotaping the spread of M&Ms, recording some of the group discussion, and taking the group's prediction as to which candidate will win the election based on its sampling.

Mr. Morales shows the video and has a student tally the group predictions on the chalkboard. The class discusses the results, the issues that were discussed in each group, how many of the groups agreed, and why their predictions were not all the same. The students decide that part of the problem was that there were too many candidates and the samples taken were too small. They discussed the primary system and the way the candidates have to be narrowed to two. They used their first count to simulate a primary election and narrowed the candidates to two. The procedure with the M&Ms was repeated, assigning several colors to each of two main candidates and taking a much larger sample to tally the results. After the sample was taken the second time, all the M&Ms were tallied to determine whether the sampling system actually predicted the election results when the sample was larger and the number of candidates narrowed. Mr. Morales then shared the results of a national opinion poll and the notation "accurate within 4 percentage points." The students then learned to compute the accuracy of their M&M poll.

As Mr. Morales shot the video documenting the procedure that the class went through to understand sampling and polls, he supplied an ongoing commentary explaining what was being done in the classroom. As a result, he has a videotape showing some of his active-learning teaching strategies that he can share with the other math teachers on his team. Since he is a math mentor teacher assigned to work with new math teachers in the district, he finds these videos valuable in helping the new teachers find ways to use practical examples in teaching students to use math applications. He also finds the videos useful in reviewing for tests in his classroom, helping students who have been absent to make up the missed assignments, and sharing concerns and celebrations with parents at parent conferences.

Classroom videos of effective teaching strategies serve as powerful tools in teacher education workshops.

Taping Practical Application Projects

In both science and math, students often fail to make connections between the topics they are studying and practical uses of these concepts and skills. Use of the camcorder to tape student projects or demonstrations of practical uses of science and math concepts and processes encourages teachers and students to make these practical uses a part of the study. One example of this is the use of slow motion photography to demonstrate science and math principles connected with athletic performance. Filming a tennis ball connecting with a tennis racket shows the importance of the placement of the racket in obtaining the best return of the ball. This particular demonstration also encourages the understanding of the interrelatedness of science and math and the use of math in calculating the timing and placement of the racket and tennis player's body to return the ball most effectively, for example.

The camcorder allows students to plan and videotape interviews of scientists and mathematicians who can explain their specialties and the science and math applications they use in their daily work. It is often eye-opening for students to see that scientists and mathematicians view reading and writing skills as vital for documenting their work. Students also have an opportunity, with an interview assignment, to see less obvious math and science connections for people in many different occupations—race car drivers, television news reporters, grocery clerks, and college professors.

Predicting and Validating

Videotaping students' predictions before a math or science activity encourages their critical thinking and activates their prior knowledge. Adding prediction to the science and math process involves several steps. First, the activity must be explained to the students, who are then given time to think about what they predict will happen. A written form for them to use in planning their predictions is shown in Figure 3.4.The students are videotaped giving their predictions as well as a short explanation of *why* they think their prediction will happen. The steps in the activity are videotaped and then viewed and discussed. The students whose predictions were correct are then videotaped explaining how they arrived at their predictions and how the process confirmed the prediction. The students whose predictions were incorrect are videotaped explaining what they learned as they were involved in the activity and why their predictions were not confirmed. These tapes can be added to the students' portfolios or used for parent conferences.

Videotaping Science and Mathematics Projects

In many schools across the country, science and math projects are completed and entered in math and science fair competitions. Because these projects are typically done at home after instruction in the classroom, one of the concerns of the teachers and judges is frequently how much of the work the students actually did.

Using the camcorder to demonstrate the steps in the research process allows the teacher to make the video available to parents so that they can see what is required and how they can support the students without doing the work for them.

F I G U R E

3.4

*Predicting
and
Validating
Form*

Project title: _____

This is what I predict will happen: _____

_____

_____

_____

Because: _____

_____

_____

_____

These are the procedures followed:

1. _____

2. _____

3. _____

4. _____

5. _____

(Continue on back, if necessary)

This is what happened: _____

_____

_____

_____

_____

My prediction was confirmed, not confirmed, because: _____

_____

_____

_____

New knowledge I gained: _____

_____

_____

_____

Videotaping outstanding projects on display at the math and science fairs also gives the teacher the opportunity to show next year's students the caliber of competition at the fairs.

Students submitting science or math projects in which each step has been documented on videotape are in unique positions to demonstrate that they used the process effectively and that they used their science or math processing skills in the way intended. By using a small video monitor in setting up their project displays, their chance of scoring well in the competition also improves; the judges have a unique ability to view the students' work and their use of the research process. Using the camcorder to support and highlight student projects involves several steps on the part of the teacher:

1. Videotape a demonstration of required steps in the project.
2. Make copies of this demonstration tape available to students and parents. This can be done easily by asking students to bring in a blank tape and having student helpers make copies of the tape. Using two VCRs with connecting cords allows you to play the tape on one VCR and copy it onto the blank tape in the other VCR. (Be careful to *play* the master tape and *record* on the blank tape. The video and audio output jacks should be used on the master tape VCR and the video and audio input jacks used on the VCR on which you are recording.)
3. Encourage students who have a camcorder at home to videotape each step of their project along with audio explaining what they are doing. Help them to plan their script and shooting schedule to make their videos more interesting and professional. For students without access to a camcorder, overnight check-out of the school camcorder can be arranged as they are ready to videotape a particular step.
4. Allow time for the students to share their projects with the class, showing their video and discussing their use of the science and math processes and the results they obtained.
5. The project videotapes can be used to demonstrate the process to next year's participants or at parent meetings or can be added to the students' portfolios. One teacher showed selections of the videos at a school board meeting at which additional video equipment was requested—and granted.

USING VIDEO TO MOTIVATE IN SCIENCE AND MATH

Video can be used to motivate students at several points in a topic of study. In the beginning, it helps students to relate their interests and background knowledge to the unit to be studied. Short video clips showing practical applications of the topic to be studied or asking questions that the students might be interested in researching help them to see the relevance of the study.

During the process of the study, video motivates students by allowing them to view themselves involved in the activities, examine their roles in group interactions, explore their assumptions, and record their predictions.

At the conclusion of the study, video allows the students to celebrate their learning, document their accomplishments, share their new understandings, and display products they have created. You may be surprised how well the students prepare for presentations just because they know they will be videotaped! Examples of the stages in video use in science and math studies are presented in Figures 3.5 and 3.6.

Guest Speakers

Guest speakers often add an element of interest to a topic and allow students to see the benefit of science and mathematics study. Videotaping the guest presentations allows the teacher to use the videos with a variety of classes over the years without having to infringe on each guest's time on a repeated basis. Of course, the guest's permission to be videotaped must be obtained before the videotape is made; it is important to explain the intended use of the videotape. Most guest speakers will be happy to oblige and if they are not comfortable being videotaped, you have at least let them know how much you value their presentation.

Guest speakers in science and math might include professionals who can explain the elements of science and math used in various occupations and professions, female scientists and mathematicians, well-known people in the community such as sports heroes or the school principal. Don't forget to contact NASA about appearances by the astronauts.

NASA Headquarters
202/358-1537

FIGURE

3.5

*Human
Body Study*

Introduction

The students are asked to name all the systems of the body and their importance to life. These lists are brainstormed and a class list is compiled.

Prestudy Use of Video

A short action video of a human body in motion is shown; the teacher stops it periodically so the students can identify any of the systems and functions previously listed on the brainstorming list and make additions and corrections as needed.

A web of the systems information is made on an overhead transparency, and the students are divided into teams to do in-depth studies of the various systems. They are instructed to do the following:

1. Use a variety of sources and find out as much as they can about the system they have been assigned.
2. Work collaboratively so that all members of the group have a job, are given equal responsibilities, and use their special talents.
3. Develop a presentation to be given to the entire class. It must include at least one demonstration and one visual.
4. Prepare for their presentation to be videotaped.

Process Use of Videotaping

As the groups are working, the teacher or video assistants videotape the group process and meet periodically with each group to view the tapes and to discuss the process and the roles the members of the groups are playing. Goals for more effective group interaction are set as the videotapes are viewed.

Culminating Use of Video

The classroom is set up for a medical seminar with the chairs arranged in a semicircular, seminar fashion. To make this day more interesting, the students are given paper lab coats as they enter the classroom. They are issued name tags and are all identified by the title *Dr.* They participate in a professional seminar and are videotaped as they give their presentations. The class members in the audience ask questions, and the teams are expected to be able to field questions about their body system.

Later the videotapes are viewed and discussed. At the conclusion of the viewing of each presentation, all students are asked to write a brief summary of the knowledge they gained from the presentation. Each group's grade is based on (1) its effectiveness working as a group, (2) the quality of its presentation, demonstration, and visual, and (3) the knowledge the rest of the class gained from its presentation. Individual students are also graded on their written responses about the body systems.

Copies of the video presentations are added to individual's video portfolios.

FIGURE

*Geometry
Study*

Introduction

Students are asked to look for geometric shapes in nature, art, and construction. A discussion of why specific shapes are chosen for specific uses is conducted with examples of aesthetics and practicality being emphasized.

Advance Organizer Video

A short video clip showing scenes of a variety of architecture can lead to a discussion of why the square and rectangle are used so much in American architecture.

Group Interactions Are Videotaped

The students are divided into teams. Their instructions follow:

1. Construct a village in which all structures needed to support village activities and the needs of the villagers are present but none of the structures may take the shape of squares or rectangles.
2. Use as many different shapes as possible in the construction. Squares and rectangles can be used for parts of the buildings but cannot be the overall shape of the building as a whole.
3. So that the measurements of your buildings can be scientifically determined, establish the scale of your buildings; and all measurements must follow the established scale. Models of the buildings must be built to scale using graph paper so that measurements can be confirmed.
4. Work together collaboratively. All members of the groups must share responsibility, and special talents of the members should be used.
5. Present your village to the class and explain how many different shapes were used, the surface and interior measurements of the structures, and how you determined these measurements.

Process Use of Videotaping

As the groups are working, the teacher or video assistants videotape the group process and meet periodically with each group to view the tapes and discuss the process and the roles the members of the groups are playing. Goals for more effective group interaction are set as the videotapes are viewed.

Culminating Use of Video

The group presentations are videotaped. After they are made, the members of the class help each group to determine the total surface of the structures constructed and the total interior room provided by their structures. These totals are charted so that the group results can be compared. Each group helps the class to discover the formula for figuring the area of the shapes used in their structures and ways to keep track of the total of the surfaces in the village as well as the interior space made available by different-shaped buildings.

Group presentation videos are copied onto individual students' video portfolios. Copies of the presentations can be used as demonstration videos for future classes.

USING VIDEO TO DOCUMENT AND CELEBRATE LEARNING

Video portfolios are very effective in demonstrating students' growing science and math skills. Each time a unit of study is explored, each student can add to her personal video portfolio through the use of an individual videotape labeled with her name. By using a sign-up sheet similar to the one illustrated in Figure 2.6 of Chapter 2, students trained to assist in videotaping in the classroom can be used to support the other students in building video portfolios.

Suggestions for building effective video portfolios include the following:

1. Train video helpers to assist in the videotaping.
2. Routinely videotape all student presentations. Let the students know that these presentations will be taped. Use the tapes to help them improve their presentation skills and set goals for themselves.
3. Tape any collaborative activities. Use the tapes to demonstrate the many roles played by members of the groups. Encourage students to refine their group interaction skills by celebrating those skills as they are demonstrated on the tapes. Segments of these group tapes can then be transferred to individual video portfolio tapes.
4. Encourage students to select from the tapes made in the classroom to include on their video portfolio tapes. A history of a project segment is a very powerful addition to a video portfolio. Help students to select segments that show their growth in concepts, processes, and collaborative roles.
5. Plan occasional interdisciplinary projects that allow students to use their unique skills in writing, drama, poetry, or art to celebrate new understandings in other curricular areas. Videotape these and include them on the video portfolio.

Using Video to Assess Skills

The use of video in assessing skills in math and science is an effective way to help students make connections between their "school learning" and real life. Show a video of a bridge being built and ask students to write about the math and science knowledge necessary in the planning and construction processes. Encourage them to make diagrams and be specific about concepts and calculations that would be necessary.

Showing a lab experiment on video and having the students write a lab procedure, hypothesis, and result report allows them to demonstrate both content and process knowledge.

With younger children, showing a time-lapse video of a seed germination and stopping the video periodically allows the students to identify the new growth demonstrated in each segment of the video. This type of assessment links the concepts and processes more closely to the students' experiences and helps them make science, math, and real-life connections.

USING VIDEO TO INVOLVE PARENTS

Since a majority of U.S. homes are now equipped with VCRs (Brock & Dodd, 1994), schools have a unique opportunity to involve parents in activities and projects through the use of video. If parents do not have access to a VCR, the school VCRs can be made available to them before and after school.

Videotapes explaining the purpose of activities and projects and helping parents to understand their role in them have been found to greatly encourage parent participation. Support for school projects greatly increases when parents understand their purposes and benefits (Forgatch & Ramsey, 1994).

Ways to use videos to help parents understand and participate more fully in their children's math and science curriculum might include the following:

1. The how and why of projects (science or math projects).
2. Helping your child with homework.
3. Encouraging budding scientists and mathematicians.
4. Tell me what you do; explain your job to your child.
5. Ways to use your camcorder to encourage your child's learning.

Explore the uses of the camcorder explained in this chapter. Make a sample tape showing an experiment with time-lapse and close-up video. Document a group interacting and a series of steps in a science or math project. As you are shooting this footage, supply audio so that people viewing the video will understand exactly what you are showing on the tape.

Evaluating and Improving Your Video

Choose a classmate or colleague and view each other's video. Critique each video and make notes about things in them that could be improved. Discuss the techniques used and how you planned for the shoot. Set goals for your next video project based on the feedback and discussion.

Video Project

Choose one of the activities described in this chapter and write a script and storyboard to implement it. Use the feedback and discussion from the practice exercise to improve your video. As you shoot the video, view the segments as you shoot them and use in-camera editing (see Appendix A, Video Resources) to replace any segments with which you are not satisfied.

PRACTICE ACTIVITY

SUMMARY

Video usage in science and math classes allows the teacher to provide a visual advance organizer as new topics are introduced, demonstrate procedures and natural phenomenon through the use of time-lapse video, close-up video, and video as observation. Making the concepts clearer in classroom demonstrations and allowing students to view actual natural occurrences with the ability to stop the video and discuss gives students opportunities to ask questions and clarify their understandings.

Science and math processes, when demonstrated on video, can be shown for review, shared with absent students when they return to school, and used to involve parents.

Classroom motivation is improved by using video at specific points in a lesson. Introducing a unit of study with video helps the students to see practical uses for the topic to be studied and activates their prior knowledge. Videotaping the students' active involvement in the classroom allows the teacher to document the students' collaborative and problem-solving skills. Documenting the culminating activities on video allows the teacher to help students improve their class presentations and interactions and celebrate their learning.

Video is effectively used in classroom assessment in several ways. Student video portfolios document the activities and growth of individuals over the course of the school year. Using videotaped experiments for student response and lab write-ups allows the teacher to closely align the assessment of the students' understanding with the actual teaching experienced in the classroom. Because science and mathematics both involve concept and process knowledge, videotaping activities in these two curricular activities are especially effective. The ability of the student to view the videotape, reflect, and self-assess becomes a valuable tool in both motivation and learning. Making demonstration and instruction videotapes available to parents encourages them to become more involved in their children's education and more supportive of current teaching methods.

REFERENCES

Ausubel, D. P. and Sullivan, E. V. (1970). *Theory and Problems of Child Development*, 2nd ed. New York: Grune & Stratton.

Brock, D., and Dodd, E. (1994). A family lending library: Promoting early literacy development. *Young Children*, *49*, 16–21.

Forgatch, M. S., and Ramsey, E. (1994). Boosting homework: A video tape link between families and schools. *School Psychology Review*, *23* (3),: 472–484.

Mullis, and Jenkins (1988, March). Making science come alive. *Science Teacher*.

SUGGESTED READINGS

Condrey, J. F. (1996, April). Focus on science concepts. *Science Teacher*.

Cwik, L. C. (1992, November/December). The camcorder as a science tool. *Science Scope,* 50–54.

Heck, J. K. (1991). Camcorders in the science classroom. *Media and Methods, 27* (4), 26–27.

Heller, N. (1994). *Projects for New Technologies in Education Grades 6–9.* Englewood, CO: Teacher Ideas Press.

Steinman, R. (1993, April). Cameras in the classroom: Tape it to the limits. *The Science Teacher*.

Camcorder Applications in the Social Sciences

A Look at the Past

Carlos and Sean stir the paint and begin to apply it to the large, flattened refrigerator box. "If this is the Old North Church, shouldn't we see if there's a picture we can go by?" asked Sean.

"I already did that," replied Carlos. "That's where I got the ideas for my sketches."

"Good!" replied Sean, "We want it to be right."

Mrs. Hamlin watches and smiles as the boys paint the church backdrop. The study of the Revolutionary War is taking on new interest. The fifth graders have read the Jean Fritz biographies of John Adams, Benjamin Franklin, King George, Samuel Adams, and Paul Revere and want to put their knowledge into a play about the American Revolution. They are planning the sets, writing the dialogue, and combining the information from all of the biographies they've read. They have even written in descriptions of ordinary citizens and how the events affected their lives. Only this morning, one of the students came into class with a copy of "The Midnight Ride of Paul Revere" as thrilled about finding it as if he had written it himself.

The script is coming along nicely. Groups of students have broken up the story into scenes and then assigned scenes to small groups of writers. The collaboration that was going on was exciting, but it was not until Mrs. Hamlin told the class that she would be videotaping the production that the students decided that the props and sets must really be done well.

The students assigned to make sets were selected by the class for their "artistic ability" and, looking pleased with themselves, had gone to the library to research pictures to be used to make sure the sets were as true-to-life as possible.

The students weren't the only ones excited about the study of the Revolution. Mrs. Hamlin thought back to the way she remembered studying history in school. Her memories of reading the chapter in the textbook and answering the questions in writing were the reason she had gone back to school to learn more about active learning strategies. She was taking a big risk with the staging of this video production. So far, it was paying off. The students enjoyed the biographies and were reading many more books voluntarily as they wrote the scripts. They were finding exciting facts, and the Jean Fritz biographies supplied little known incidents of the Revolution.

Mrs. Hamlin smiles to herself as Jeannette comes up to her with the latest revision of the script for King George. "He really didn't understand the colonists' viewpoint," said Jeannette. "We want to make sure that the script helps the audience to understand that, especially since we're making the video and many other people will get to see our play. We really want it to be good."

"Let me read it to you aloud. You listen and see how well you've captured his viewpoint," replies Mrs. Hamlin solemnly.

The Washington High School students in Mr. Howard's twentieth century history class are discussing the use of the Internet in researching their video documentaries. One of the students has been able to access the Internet and use the Video Encyclopedia of the Twentieth Century to insert video clips into his documentary.

"These are actual film clips from the newsreels of the day," Michael explains as he relates his experiences on the Internet. "Mr. Lawson in the media center showed me how to access the encyclopedia. Now I can use the actual film from the day to show the sequence of events I want to show in my documentary. It's much more powerful than simulations, although I will still use some of those, too."

Mr. Howard smiles, "I'm glad Mr. Lawson was able to show you how to do that. Film clips from newsreels will really add interest to your documentary! Especially since you're documenting the history of the airplane in this century. The newsreels will show how rapidly their designs and uses changed!"

"That's what I discovered. It's easier to see on the film clips. Otherwise, I was going to have to use models or still photos. The video and movement is much more effective."

Each person's contribution to a play is documented by making a videotape such as "The Production of a Historic Play."

CHAPTER OBJECTIVES

As Mrs. Hamlin and Mr. Howard have discovered, students can be motivated to study a topic in great depth when their intellectual curiosity is aroused with unique projects. The social sciences are particularly intriguing when students are given opportunities to view history, geography, politics, and even economics through the eyes of citizens of a different time or place. Integrating the language and visual arts into projects adds an additional element by allowing students with unique talents and intelligence strengths to interpret the social sciences in innovative ways. The purpose of this chapter is to support the use of video and active learning in the teaching of the social sciences. By reading this chapter and completing the video practice activity you will learn

1. To use video to enrich instruction in history, geography, sociology, anthropology, and economics.
2. To use video to motivate students to become more actively involved in the social sciences.
3. To use video to document and celebrate students' progress in social science content, processes, and applications.
4. To help parents understand innovative teaching strategies and how to support their children's learning.

USING VIDEO TO TEACH THE SOCIAL SCIENCES

There are many disciplines to integrate in the teaching of social sciences. History, geography, political science, and economics are just a few of the aspects of social science that, along with the study of art, music, drama, and dance of the period being studied, interact to support the students' understanding of times past as well as currently evolving events. Although field trips to actual historic places as well as museums might be the best choice for giving students rich experience in the social sciences and arts, video often is the most practical choice.

In the area of geography, maps and globes have been the traditional visuals most frequently used. Maps are valuable resources, and teaching map skills is vital in helping students to understand the locations of countries, cities, oceans, rivers, lakes, and mountains. If, however, the students have never seen an ocean or a mountain, viewing video of these is important to their visualization of map features. Video made by the teacher or parents in the class can add valuable context to the lessons being taught. A video showing a mountain and the teacher climbing it, showing the rocks and flowers, and indicating the effort involved in climbing is much more valuable in having the students understand the size and features of a mountain than any professional video. Showing the color coding of the mountain on a map also allows comparison with higher mountains and visualization by the students of how much more difficult it might be to climb the higher mountains. This information can then be related to a study of the westward movement and the difficulty in moving covered wagons across mountains or of any other period in history for which perseverance and movement across natural obstacles is important to understand.

When studying particular periods of history, video can be used to present the art and music of the period, social customs, and reenactments of famous plays of the time. Going even farther, video clips of the way business was conducted, the roles of women and minorities, and everyday life help students to understand more about what it was like to live during a period of history. To support this approach to the study of history, books like *A Pioneer Sampler: The Daily Life of a Pioneer Family in 1840*

Using video scenes of geographic features in conjunction with instruction in reading maps helps students to visualize the coding on the maps as mountains, rivers, oceans, and other natural phenomena.

by Barbara Greenwood help students to understand the lives of ordinary people and are helpful in supporting students in writing scripts for video reenactments.

Using video to teach the social sciences involves the collection of video clips to illustrate important aspects of study, and this takes time. You can build this video teaching library in the following ways:

- Collecting video from vacation trips. (Ask your accountant about possible tax benefits to you.)
- Borrowing video from parents, friends, and neighbors. (Make copies so they can be included in your video teaching library.)
- Videotaping clips from television news shows, PBS shows, and other television programs. (As a rule of thumb, these tapes can be retained and used for 45 days after broadcast and then must be destroyed unless wider permission to use is obtained from the broadcast company. See tips on copyright in Appendix B, Teacher Resources for more information.)
- Saving copies of your students' video projects over the years. (See tips on storing and preserving video in the Appendix A, Video Resources).

Teaching Participation Skills

Teaching participation skills in the social sciences is particularly vital but often neglected in today's schools. According to the California Department of Education (1988) *participation skills* are defined as the skills necessary for individuals to successfully contribute to the good of the community; they include three types of attributes.

Personal Skills
- Sensitivity to others.
- Understanding of yourself.
- Communicating well.
- Being aware of bias, prejudice, and stereotyping.
- Adjusting to the needs of others to work as an effective group member.

Group Interaction Skills

- Listening to the views of others.
- Participating in decision making in a group setting.
- Leading and following in group settings.
- Persuading, compromising, debating, and negotiating.
- Working within a group while maintaining group relations.

Social and Political Participation Skills

- Identifying issues.
- Committing to social responsibilities.
- Working to influence those in political power.
- Being willing to accept responsibility and the consequences of your own actions.

"While the ability to work with others is an asset in any society, it is a requirement for citizenship in a democracy" (California Department of Education, 1988, p. 24). Participation skills must first be taught and practiced in collaboration projects within the classroom and can then be expanded to service learning projects in the community. Teaching participation skills in a climate of mistrust of the political systems and leaders is not an easy job. The students may not have seen their parents modeling participation and will need to be introduced to the basic ways in which an informed electorate participates in government.

Video can be a big help in visually demonstrating these roles to students. Take your camcorder with you when you go to the poll on election day. Provide a commentary as you approach the polling place. Talk about the fact that polls are located in non-threatening places, such as public buildings and, in some states, private homes. At the polling place, film the sign and the notice about not placing campaign signs close to a polling place. Try to arrive at the poll at a time when you can interview the people working there. Explain off camera that you are making a video to show your class about the right to vote.

When showing the video to your class, discuss the importance of voting, the volunteers and their role in running the polling places, and all the aspects of the right to vote, such as the responsibility to be knowledgeable about the issues and the people who are running for office. Videotaping some of the political commercials ahead of time will also give students an opportunity to be informed consumers. Many of the commercials contradict each other. Ask students what other sources of information are available to make good decisions. This question encourages research on ways to obtain voting records and information about patterns of voting and support of candidates for key issues. During election years, you, as the teacher, have unique opportunities to build your video teaching library with video of political rallies, political conventions, election night returns, and so on. Video of evolving current events can be used to spark discussion, to simplify and illustrate the process, and to assist with assessment, as will be discussed later in the chapter.

The importance of participation in society should not be limited to the political arena, however. Citizenship projects such as recycling, neighborhood clean-up, graffiti clean-up, and planting and beautification projects are very effective in demonstrating the role of volunteers in maintaining the quality of life in a free society. Service learning projects help students to experience the exhilaration of sharing in a large project, which is easily done when a group of people work together. The videos made before, during, and after the project and viewed at the culmination celebration help students to see the value of their participation as well as the concrete results of their labor. This video can be saved for use with future groups as they begin to select projects and to see the benefits of participation.

One student collaboration project that fosters understanding among the diverse cultural groups within a classroom is a social studies video project in which students with different linguistic and cultural groups are placed in groups to work on a documentary about their native country. The student whose native country is the focus of the documentary becomes the "content expert" and the group plans a video project highlighting the country of the content expert's birth. The group decides together which aspects of the geography, music, art, culture, economics, government, and so on will be highlighted. The group writes a script, gathers artifacts, obtains guest speakers and photographs from the country, and prepares a storyboard and videotaping schedule. The teacher must approve the script and storyboard and help the group refine its plans before the project is videotaped. The group videotapes the project using a student videographer and then the class views and critiques the result. These videos become a part of the school library video collection and can be used by other teachers throughout the school, so it is very important that the efforts of all the students involved be recognized in the closing credits (Heath, 1996).

Teaching Critical Thinking Skills

The abilities to define and clarify problems, judge information related to a problem, and solve problems and reach conclusions are among the most difficult things to teach. Although these are very high-level thinking skills, the concepts involved must be built over the years, beginning in the primary grades, if students are to become skilled in critical thinking. Many primary grade teachers have found that using television commercials to help young students understand the persuasion approaches used in sales helps them to use judgment in making decisions. Teaching critical thinking often involves discussing of problems from various viewpoints. Using situational videos can be very useful in sparking discussion. Videotaping clips from newscasts on television or even situation comedies can give the students practice in viewing conflict from various points of view.

Practice in listening to the views of others and use of logic to sway others to a person's own point of view can be staged with the benefit of a videotaped situation of a problem. If the situation or problem also makes the students aware of current events or societal concerns, it becomes even more compelling. Debates over issues introduced in this way also give students practice in researching facts, preparing background information, and presenting their arguments in logical fashion.

As was discussed in Chapter 2, videotaping the debates, discussions, and group interactions as cooperation and collaboration are practiced, and then viewing the videos and discussing the quality of the interactions and roles of the participants often give the students a clearer picture of their own interaction skills. Setting goals for future debates and collaborations helps the students to practice and master the interpersonal communication skills necessary for effective exchange of ideas and consensus building.

Teaching Basic Study Skills

"The most basic skills of the history-social science fields involve obtaining information and judging its value, reaching reasoned conclusions based on the evidence and developing sound judgment" (California Department of Education, 1988, p. 26). Very often the resources available to students in our schools are limited only by the imagination and ingenuity of the teachers. Yes, school libraries often have small collections, but often many other resources are available to students. Public libraries, college libraries, historical societies, public records, and private foundations often hold historical collections that can be exciting resources for young historians and researchers. As you, the teacher, research the possibilities of community resources, take your camcorder along. The librarians and historians you find will be grateful that you are preparing an introduction for your students. As you receive an orientation to the facilities and the rules, videotape the presentation so that your students will know where to go, whom to talk to, and what services are available to them. In other words, use the video to introduce knowledge of the facilities to the students. Most librarians are gracious in giving help but do not want to have to do a basic orientation on an individual basis. In addition, the students are much more likely to use the facilities once they have an understanding of the location and rules. You may even be able to entrust older, more responsible students with making the orientation videos. Again, once made, these videos become a part of your teaching video collection. A similar video, made in your own school library, can be used to orient new students who enter school after the beginning of the school year. Parents often find these orientation videos valuable, too.

USING VIDEO TO MOTIVATE LEARNING IN THE SOCIAL SCIENCES

Making videos to simulate history is one of the ways in which to motivate students in studying the social sciences. A historical simulation video involves a number of the social science competencies. Researching the events in history in order to write the

*Literature for History-
Social Science,
Kindergarten–Grade Eight*
(1993)
Publication #1107
California Department of
Education
Bureau of Publications,
Sales Unit
P.O.Box 271
Sacramento, CA 95812-
0271
1-800-995-4099

script, working together collaboratively to plan props and back-drops, and making decisions about who should play the parts and how the video should be edited involve complex social interactions. Research involves not just the historical events but also the costumes, language, and sets of the period being presented.

An effective way to begin video projects depicting historical events is through the use of a piece of historical literature. The students first read it and then rewrite it in script form, choosing the scenes that most graphically depict the events of the story and its place in history. The language, settings, props, and costumes still must be researched, but often the piece of literature itself includes some assistance in these areas. The California Department of Education publishes a helpful booklet that will assist you in finding good historical literature.

Video Tips for Historical Simulation Videos

Indoor scenes in historical simulations provide a challenge for students to research the furnishings, costumes, and availability of technology—electricity, telephones, and so on—of the time being documented. Large cardboard boxes painted to represent historic rooms make good sets and give artistic students an opportunity to become important to the production.

For outdoor scenes, whenever possible shoot in outside locations that are "neutral," such as in a park with many trees, in a remote area outside the city perhaps, and on unpaved roads and foot trails. Choosing these kinds of environments—similar to those that existed at all times in recorded history—will allow more freedom in shooting. Make sure to avoid signs of modern life: people in modern dress, telephone poles, tire tracks, soft drink cans and other litter, and so on. Use nature whenever possible: birds, close-ups of tree branches and wild flowers, and large expanses of blue sky that you can pan the camera across and meet the sun for a nice effect.

If you are shooting persons who are narrating—telling the story to the camera as if to another person—situate them in a plain room against a neutral background. Light them with a couple of stand lamp fixtures, and videotape them in a medium close-up. This set-up is particularly effective when you want your audience's close attention.

When changing scenes and to indicate the passage of time, you can use the fade-to-black feature that is standard equipment on most camcorders. Be sure to fade in from black when you shoot the next image.

A good technique for moving from the narrator to another scene is to use a *rack-focus.* As you move from the narrator, turn the focus ring on the camcorder to a point at which the narrator's image is totally blurred as he concludes talking. Then set up the next scene, start the camera rolling, and bring the scene into sharp focus.

If your characters can move within a frame and you want to show passage of time, have them leave the frame from either camera left or right and then have them reenter in the next scene from the opposite screen direction. For example, Thomas Jefferson, having had his say about independence, rises from the table upon which he has been writing, and exits screen left. Let the camera roll for a few seconds without Jefferson in the scene, fade to black, and then pause or stop the recording. Set up the next scene, fade in from black, roll camera for a few seconds on the empty set, and then cue Jefferson to enter, this time from screen right. The impression is that he left the location, went away for awhile (perhaps even to Paris) and, at last, has come back to resume his profound thinking about his country's future. In the viewer's eye, Jefferson has been gone for months, when actually all the real time it took was 10 minutes, enough time for him to change costume and walk back into the scene from the opposite direction.

Some commonly used, perhaps overused, passage of time transitions include zooming in on a ticking clock face, rack-focusing, changing the hands of a clock and then refocusing on the new time, flipping the pages of a calendar that has been set on a music stand or easel, tilting the camera up toward the sun, rack-focusing and then focusing back on a nighttime scene, just to name a few. Another is a "swish pan," as described in Chapter 1, a quick lateral move of the camcorder from point A to point B, usually as a transition.

For other transitions, choose certain important points in the story and find or make illustrations, objects, or symbols that will represent those story segments. If you are telling the story of

Betsy Ross, have a female voice narrate the story off camera while you slowly zoom into an illustration of the famous seamstress stitching the flag. Or use a flag by arranging it so that only the stripes show (you don't want too many stars in this picture!) and shoot hands sewing in medium close-up.

Begin and end your historical segments with pictures, objects, or illustrations that are appropriate to the period of history that you are covering. The images can be symbolic, rather than literal to the story. An American eagle or the U.S. flag shot from an imaginative angle can represent volumes of U.S. history.

Use sound effects to emphasize certain points in your historical narrative. There are copyright-free music and sound effect CDs available (see the listing of suppliers in Appendix B, Teacher Resources), or you can experiment with your own, either prerecorded and played back on a cassette near the camcorder or produced live while shooting the video.

Involving the students in the production of the video as director, camerapersons, set designers, and prop persons is highly motivational. These videos can be copied, included in individual students' video portfolios, and even used in future classes as teaching devices. A "history of the production video" made by the teacher or student assistant provides opportunities to examine the planning and interpersonal skills of the students involved in the production. This type of video is also a good way to show parents the skills, research, and learning that takes place when students are involved in active learning projects.

Using a video of actual news footage of a conflict situation shown on television news is a good way for students to examine the behaviors and communications that sometimes cause problems. First viewing the news footage, discussing what kinds of actions would possibly have changed the outcomes, and then role-playing the more positive interactions often help students to see the impact of positive personal interactions, listening to the viewpoints of others, or even researching background and responding with more knowledge. A video made of the role-playing can then be compared to news footage. The personal skills needed to make positive outcomes occur can then be discussed.

In the early grades, the traditional study unit, *Our Family*, expanded to include a look at the family history, provides an opportunity to introduce many of the social sciences. In the beginning of this study, you may want to read a series of books about the ways in which family histories are maintained. Some examples include *The Keeping Quilt* by Patricia Polacco and *Knots on a Counting Rope* by Bill Martin, Jr., and John Archambault. Discussing the reasons why families keep family histories helps the students to determine why they would want to participate in a family history project and to help them determine who they need to interview and what information they will collect. Asking students to interview members of their families helps them to gain a comprehensive understanding of the reasons that people make decisions and change jobs or locations. Interviews with parents and grandparents help support the concepts of time sequence, factors that influence the sequence of events and change, and an awareness of the impact of world events, economics, and geography in relation to personal decisions. Preparing students to conduct interviews of family members is an important aspect of this type of assignment. Preparing questions ahead of time and practice in interviewing are essential factors in this assignment. Videotaping and viewing and discussing practice interviews helps the students to become more confident before they actually conduct the interviews on camera. Emphasizing the discovery of the background of the family, where they lived, whether they lived in other parts of the country or world, and then showing any travel or movement that occurred using maps or even video simulations make the project more interesting and informative. Researching the costumes and customs of the time, often using information obtained during the interviews, helps to make the video simulations come alive. A planning guide for use in preparing the interviews and preparing the visuals and video is helpful to the students. See Figure 4.1 for an example.

Special event videos often serve as introductions to topics of study in the social sciences. Viewing footage from the Olympics, for example, leads naturally into a study of the origins of the games and how the games have changed over time. The impact of politics and world events on the games provides an opportunity to study world history, politics, and even economics (how were the games financed?). A study of the impact of technology

FIGURE

4.1

*Family
History
Planning
Guide*

Why do you think it is important to find out more about your family?

What new information do you hope to find?

Whom will you interview? (List everyone you plan to interview.)

Name   Questions Prepared   Questions Sent to Them   Interview Set Up

What questions will you ask?

Don't forget to ask:

Where did the family originate?
What movements have been made? When?

What other sources of information will you use?

Family Bible   Family photo albums   Other _____

How will you present your findings?

Props needed:

Maps needed:

Costumes needed:

Planning checklist:

_____ Script written

_____ Sequence of video shots planned

_____ Storyboard completed

on all aspects of the games—the timing, scoring, television transmission—supports the students' understanding of technology and ways in which it affects communication and understanding between the peoples of the world. The class may then want to stage its own version of the Olympics, giving members an opportunity to research the countries they want to represent. Which events are likely to be strong in given countries? How does the geography, terrain, and life style of the people of different countries affect the sports? How do the values of the people and government influence their participation in the Olympic Games? The whole research process should be videotaped. The students are then given an opportunity to view the decision making, planning, and interactions as their project builds. A final video for this project might involve oral presentations on the countries involved, including their flags, geography, and athletic strengths. The class version of the Olympics might include some new events and provide an opportunity to introduce some unknown sports, innovative ways of timing and scoring, uses of math and science in the Olympics, and even simulated newscasts—a way to integrate writing skills.

Using Video Simulations

Video simulations offer endless possibilities for in-depth research, writing, and video production in the social sciences. Storyboards would be useful on these simulations if it is important that specific shots are included. A shooting script or outline normally suffices for the active simulations, but the videographer should be aware of the sequence of activity so that she can shoot in a relatively narrow area and follow the one or two students most likely to fulfill the object of the simulation. If the object of the simulation is to produce a model video, the teacher and students should thoroughly plan and preproduce sequences wanted and shoot the simulation "film-style," scene by scene until an acceptable finished product is achieved. Some examples of simulations follow:

A simulation of gold fever provides a personal understanding for students studying this period of history. This is an example of a simulation that could be shot with a minimum of preproduction. The videographer should be aware of the kinds of actions likely to occur and be following one or two students to capture their reactions and interactions.

One teacher discovered during a discussion of the Gold Rush that her students thought gold fever was a disease that the forty-niners caught while they were out in the wilderness searching for gold. She planned a simulation of gold fever by spray painting rocks with gold paint and hiding the rocks throughout the classroom, while the students were at recess. As they returned to the classroom she gave them each a piece of yarn with which to "stake their claim" when they discovered gold. She then videotaped what happened as they entered the room and searched for gold. Their frenzied rushing from place to place, their reluctance to leave the area once they surrounded their gold with their yarn, the arguments that occurred when more than one "miner" discovered gold at the same time were all captured on tape. Once all the gold was discovered, the teacher sat the students down and they viewed the videotape together so the students could see how much their behavior changed during the search for gold. They then expanded the discussion to the term gold fever. The students understood the term better because they had experienced it, both in person and on video. They continued the study by researching the topic more fully and writing essays on gold fever, what it meant, and how it affected the actions, movements, and decisions made by the forty-niners.

A simulated wagon train activity starts with research on the length of the trip, supplies needed and their availability along the way, and the size and construction of the wagons used. The

Classroom simulations such as "Gold Fever" allow students to experience the frenzy and then view themselves exhibiting the fever.

dress of the period is also researched as well as the more common wagon train routes.

Simulations of the supplies and costumes are created using cardboard and recycled materials. A script and storyboard for a video documenting the journey are prepared, and the simulation video is made.

A simulated wagon is laid out in a part of the classroom and the simulated supplies are packed on it. The family and others going on the trip are videotaped as they discuss their plans and the ways in which they make decisions about packing the wagons. Which things must be readily available? Where is everyone going to ride and sleep? The trip is depicted with the use of script and maps showing the length of time spent on the journey. Occasional scenes of the family are shown to depict the new concerns and planning as they run out of supplies or have to make changes because of obstacles they encounter during the trip. The sequence is videotaped and available to be viewed and discussed by the class, parents, and administrators. The video becomes a part of the teacher's library of teaching videos. One class experience can then be shared with future classes who may choose to simulate another experience in the social sciences.

A simulation of the building of the pyramids also must begin with extensive research (see *Pyramid* by David Macaulay), the writing of a script and storyboard, and a simulation of the events. The sequence described for the wagon train simulation is then followed. Once the preproduction research and planning are finished, the simulation is videotaped and the tape shared and discussed.

Historical Reenactments

Historical reenactments also offer a wide variety of opportunities. These must be carefully researched to provide the proper language, costume, and setting with a brief historical background.

> *Famous speeches:* Kennedy's inaugural address, Lincoln's Gettysburg Address, Nixon's resignation speech.
>
> *Famous events:* the signing of the Declaration of Independence or the Magna Carta and the Moon Landing.
>
> *Famous incidents:* Rosa Parks on the bus in Alabama, the suffragettes, the presidential assassinations.

Videotaping oral presentations of historical reenactments provides a motivation to prepare thoroughly and gives the student an opportunity to view his own presentation and set goals for future presentations. The use of videotaped presentations for self-evaluation will be discussed later in the chapter.

Current Events

The study of current events provides a natural video possibility. A daily, biweekly, or weekly newscast of current events broadcast throughout the school or taped and circulated throughout the school is an outstanding way to motivate the reading of newspapers, the researching of background information for newscasts, and the writing of news stories. Using students as production crew on a rotating basis provides a wealth of experience. School events provide opportunities for writing and asking interview questions, spotlighting key school personnel, and even producing commercials for the school store or cafeteria. Several schools have written grants that have provided editing equipment and additional camcorders for use in newscast programming. See Chapter 6 for a more in-depth discussion of implementing school newscasts.

USING VIDEO TO DOCUMENT AND CELEBRATE LEARNING

Videos placed in individual student portfolios provide a way to visually demonstrate learning that is taking place. Because so many of the social science objectives emphasize personal skills, research skills, group interaction skills, and social and political participation skills as well as content, video is a good choice to demonstrate the use of these process skills and growth in personal interactions. Videos made for projects in class are a good source for short clips to be used in personal portfolios.

The videotaping of oral presentations gives the student presenting an opportunity to view the tape and do some self-evaluation. Once the student has viewed the tape, the teacher and student can use the presentation to analyze the research done and the presentation skills and then set goals for future reports.

The student has a much more concrete idea of strengths and areas to improve having seen the presentation on tape. The tape can then become a part of the student's portfolio and be used to demonstrate growth at a later date when an additional presentation is given and videotaped, and a comparison of the two tapes can be made. Using a scoring rubric for the oral presentations is helpful for students to see what is expected and what can be done to improve future presentations. Figure 4.2 shows an example of a scoring rubric. It is helpful for the student to self-evaluate using the rubric and then compare the self-evaluation with the teacher's evaluation on the same rubric.

As has been mentioned previously in this chapter, using video for goal setting is an effective way to involve the students in self-evaluation and personal goal setting. Using video taped periodically throughout the year helps the student to see the progress that is being made and strive to improve even further. Video often

F I G U R E   *Sample Scoring Rubric for Oral Presentations*
4.2

Research

Research incomplete or false information given	Research fairly complete	Research complete	Research well done	Research outstanding; little-known facts given
	Important facts left out			

Visuals

No visuals used	Visual used but poorly done	Good visual	Visual very good, helped listeners to understand	Visual outstanding, innovative

Presentation Skills

Read notes	Used notes too much	Had notes available, used very little	Spoke without notes	Spoke without notes, obviously knew material well

Little eye contact – Much eye contact
Spoke too softly – Used good projection

provides an opportunity for students with visual, musical, or kinesthetic intelligence to demonstrate their understanding in innovative ways. Giving students an opportunity to choose ways to demonstrate their understandings by designing props and scenery for a historical reenactment of simulation activity or a series of political posters makes the study come alive for individual students with unique talents but also strengthens the knowledge of the other students in the classroom. Including projects such as researching and teaching the sports or dances of the time period being studied provides the same kind of in-depth understanding as does a display of the famous art of the period or a demonstration and discussion of the music of the time.

Video used for assessment purposes in the social sciences provides the teacher with an actual event or interaction about which the students can write, demonstrating their understanding of the complexities of social incidents and their knowledge of problem-solving strategies. The use of a video to spark discussion also gives the teacher an opportunity to evaluate students' abilities to understand situations, express their beliefs, and suggest solutions. A scoring rubric similar to the one used for scoring oral presentations can be prepared prior to this type of exercise so that the teacher can score participants easily. See Figure 4.3 for an example.

F I G U R E 4.3   *Scoring Rubric for Video Problem-Solving Exercise*

Understanding of Problem

Misunderstands problem or cause	Little understanding of problem, incomplete understanding of the cause	Understands problem superficially	Complete understanding of problem & cause

Ability to Communicate

Difficulty communicating	Communicates minimally	Communicates well	Outstanding communication

Problem-Solving Ability

No solutions presented	Simplistic solutions offered	Possible solutions offered	Innovative solutions offered, more than one given based on assumptions

USING VIDEO TO INVOLVE PARENTS

In today's society, many parents own camcorders and VCRs and can be very helpful in providing video to be added to the teaching video library. Vacation video of historical places, interesting geographic features, or past events in family history are often a part of parents' video libraries. Making them aware of your interest in building a video teaching library may help them to evaluate their own video libraries and provide tapes that could be copied and added to the class library.

Preparing videos of class activities for parent use provides the parents with a deeper understanding of the projects and teaching methods being used in the social science classroom. Videotapes showing the importance of participation and study skills in the classroom and ways that these same skills can be improved in the home situation will serve to involve the parents in working as a part of the instructional team. Instructional videos for parents that demonstrate ways for them to support their children's learning make it easier for parents and teachers to communicate and work together. Multiple copies of these videos made available for parent viewing also serve as a positive interaction between school and home.

If a major project is being required of the students, a video showing the steps in preparing the project, possible examples of projects done in the past, and communicating the expectations are very helpful for parents.

Other possible topics for parent involvement videos include the following:

- Community resources available for student research.
- Sources of props, costumes, and "junk" for student projects.
- Setting up a study area in the home; ways to encourage good study habits.
- Suggestions for preparing effective oral reports.

PRACTICE ACTIVITY

As a part of the process of planning to use video in the classroom, prepare a class presentation and videotape it as you, the teacher, present it. Prepare a scoring rubric or use one of the ones provided in this chapter to score your presentation and set goals for yourself based on the videotape. Use the tape and evaluation to demonstrate to your class how they will be videotaped, self-evaluate, and set goals with you, the teacher. Make this video a part of your video teaching library for future use.

Evaluating and Improving Your Video

Go back to Chapter 1 and evaluate the video you made in the video practice activity based on the guidelines given there. Is your video in focus? Have you allowed effective head room? Is the composition pleasing? Note the ways in which the video can be improved and emphasize those factors as you complete your video project for this chapter.

Video Project

After you have used the video of your own class presentation, assign an oral presentation to your class. Be sure that the presentation involves students researching a topic and preparing a visual of some kind to make the presentation interesting. The scoring rubric you will use to evaluate their presentations should be discussed with the students before they make their presentations. Videotape the presentations, allow the students to view and evaluate their own presentations, and then identify a goal or goals that they would like to work toward. Store the tapes in the students' portfolios for future use. The following are some suggestions for projects:

- Research a state or country and present your research in video format. Include photographs, artwork, artifacts, and guest expert interviews when possible.
- Research a time in history and present an original "day in the life of an average citizen" of the time. Highlight the way life was different in those days, the clothing worn in the period, daily activities, and how citizens managed without the use of modern conveniences.
- Prepare a documentary of an event in history including both situations that led up to the event and the impact of the event itself. Use photographs or video clips if available to tell the story and focus on the people who played major parts in the event and their roles.
- Plan a video project based on a current event. Include video clips from television newscasts and include any controversy surrounding the event. You might include a group discussion or debate showing the different opinions regarding the event, a news article that appeared in print media, the opinion of "the person on the street," or other devices to show the opinions of the people. This project can be based on a school, local, regional, or national event.

SUMMARY

Teaching the social sciences involves not only content but also several personal skills, interactive skills, and research skills. Video is a natural way to provide context in the form of visual examples, to document the students' growing personal, interactive, and research skills as they engage in active learning activities in the classroom, and provide real-life problems from television newscast video.

The teacher has an opportunity to integrate many social science disciplines in the classroom through the use of video. Helping support the student's understanding of the interactions of language, art, music, clothing, and values in different historical periods is an effective use of video in the social sciences.

The study of map and globe skills using video of the landmarks being located on the map or globe helps the student to visualize the real landmark represented by symbols.

The participation by students in civic responsibilities is encouraged with the use of video. Being able to see the process of registering to vote, researching the issues, and actually going to the polling place via video makes the process more familiar and accessible. Service learning projects videotaped from start to finish provide the students with proof of the value of their participation.

The planning and participation in active learning projects is greatly enhanced when the projects are videotaped, viewed, and celebrated. Oral presentations, when videotaped, can be used to encourage self-evaluation and goal setting by students. Placing the video records of the student projects into individual portfolios allows the students, parents, and teacher to evaluate growth and goal achievement over time.

Parent involvement is encouraged by building a video teaching library that may include contributions from parent video libraries and vacation video showing historical landmarks, interesting land forms and features, or current events. Videos available for parent use to support learning at home, explain unique project requirements, or suggest ways to improve study habits are valuable ways to encourage school-home interactions.

CHILDREN'S BOOKS CITED

Fritz, J. (1977). *Can't You Make Them Behave, King George?* New York: Coward-McCann.

Fritz, J. (1976). *What's the Big Idea, Ben Franklin?* New York: Coward-McCann.

Fritz, J. (1975). *Where Was Patrick Henry on the 29th of May?* New York: Coward-McCann.

Fritz, J. (1974). *Why Don't You Get a Horse, Sam Adams?* New York: Coward-McCann.

Greenwood, B. (1994). *A Pioneer Sampler: The Daily Life of a Pioneer Family in 1840.* Boston, MA: Houghton-Mifflin.

Macauley, D. (1975). *Pyramid.* New York: The Trumpet Club, Houghton Mifflin.

Martin, B., and Archambault, J. (1987). *Knots on a Counting Rope.* New York: Henry Holt and Co.

Polacco, P. (1988). *The Keeping Quilt.* New York: Simon and Schuster.

REFERENCES

California Department of Education (1988). *History/Social Science Framework.* Sacramento, CA: California Department of Education.

Heath, I. A. (1996, May/June). The social studies video project: A holistic approach for teaching linguistically and culturally diverse students. *The Social Studies.*

SUGGESTED READINGS

Anderson, G., and Balog, P. (1994, Jan/Feb). Equipment for in-school broadcasting studios. *Media and Methods,* 15–17.

Baraloto, R. A., and Silvious, S, (1991). 1+1+30= Instructional Success. *School Library Media Activities Monthly, 7* (1), 36–38.

Baraloto, R. A., and Silvious, S. (1992). VCR: A new emphasis on the "C" in the classroom curriculum. *School Library Media Activities Monthly, 7* (8), 37–39.

Beasley, A. (1993). *Looking Great With Video.* Worthington, OH: Linwood Publishing.

Beasley, A. E. (1994). The camcorder revolution. *School Library Media Activities Monthly, 10* (5), 38–39+.

Beasley, A. E. 1994. Creating documentaries. *School Library Media Activities Monthly, 10* (9), 38–41.

Elias, M., and Taylor, M. (1995, Spring). Building social and academic skills via problem solving videos. *Teaching Exceptional Children.*

Heller, N. (1994). *Projects for New Technologies in Education Grades 6–9.* Englewood, CO: Teacher Ideas Press.

Sinofsky, E. R. (1994). *A Copyright Primer for Educational and Industrial Media Producers.* Washington, DC: Copyright Information Services.

Camcorder Applications in Physical Education and the Visual and Performing Arts

Picture This

Play practice is not going well. Miss Adams looks at Mr. Johannsen and whispers, "Is it too late to cancel this production?"

None of the high school students involved in the play seem to have any life left in them. It is late in the year, it is hot, and opening night is only two weeks away. Miss Adams watches as Mr. Johannsen gets up and walks out of the auditorium. She thinks to herself, "Oh no! He's walking out on me!"

A few minutes later she sees movement out of the corner of her eye and realizes that it's her coproducer returning. As she turns around to watch him, she realizes he's setting up a camcorder and tripod. Miss Adams chuckles to herself, "What a good idea!"

After the practice session, the actors and stage hands gather in the front rows of the auditorium to watch the video of the last act of the play. "Before I show this video, I want you to know why I taped the practice," Mr. Johannsen says quietly. "There's no energy in your practice. I want you to watch yourself and think about how your character comes across. If you are a stagehand, watch the things you're responsible for. This showing is for you to find ways to improve your own performance, not to criticize others. Tomorrow I'll videotape again, and you can see for yourself whether your performance is getting any better. I'll give you suggestions tomorrow. Today, I want you to think for yourself and set one goal for tomorrow."

As the video is shown, the room grows very quiet. Occasionally, one of the actors groans softly but other than those quiet sounds, there is focused attention.

At the conclusion of the video, Miss Adams is standing at the front of the stage with 3" × 5" cards in her hand. "Now take a card," she says. "Write down your one goal for tomorrow's practice and give it to me before you leave."

As the actors and stagehands leave the auditorium, there is a steady hum of upbeat conversation. "I know exactly what I need to do tomorrow," one of the lead actors whispers to Miss Adams. "The old saying 'a picture is worth a thousand words' is sure true!"

"Picture this!" says her costar. "Tomorrow my character is actually going to be played as a living being!"

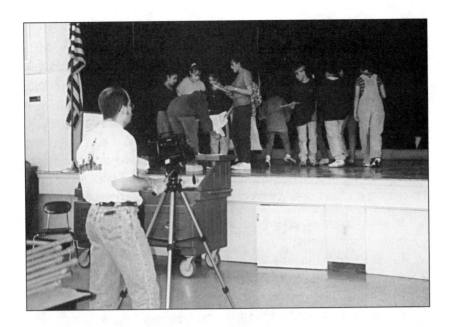

Videotaping play practice helps the actors to improve their performance. Videotaping the actual performance provides footage for their individual portfolios.

CHAPTER OBJECTIVES

As Miss Adams and Mr. Johannsen discovered, students are not always aware of how they are moving and performing. This self-knowledge is never more important than in physical education and the visual and performing arts. Professionals in these areas have long used video to analyze and perfect their art. This chapter shows ways that video can be used in educating and training young performers to make them more aware of their movements and help them find ways to improve their performance. By reading this chapter and completing the video practice activity, you will learn

1. To use video to enrich instruction in physical education and the visual and performing arts.
2. To use video to motivate students to become more actively involved in physical education and the visual and performing arts.
3. To use video to document and celebrate students' progress.
4. To help parents understand the innovative teaching strategies now being used in schools and to support their children's learning.

USING VIDEO TO TEACH PHYSICAL EDUCATION AND THE VISUAL AND PERFORMING ARTS

Teaching in physical education and the visual and performing arts has always been done in the active mode. It is impossible to instruct in movement, dance, theater, music, or art without giving the student practice in the movements and techniques being taught. It could be argued that students must have some basic talents in the skills and techniques being taught. This may be true, but the objectives of these areas of instruction speak to basic levels of competence that make all students physically and artistically educated. Howard Gardner's research in multiple intelligences (1993) found that all human beings have seven intelligences—in varying levels, of course.

In the artistic and movement studies the musical, spatial/visual, and kinesthetic intelligences are employed in addition to the linguistic and logical/mathematical ones that are more commonly involved in school-related curriculum.

The goal of this chapter is to find ways to give all students a chance to enhance all seven intelligences and succeed in physical education and the visual and performing arts. Even if they cannot dance on Broadway, they should at least be comfortable and confident enough to participate in school dances and be able to socialize with others without feeling awkward, for example. The use of video in teaching physical education and the arts helps heighten the musical, visual, and kinesthetic intelligences; makes students more aware of their movements; and gives them confidence in their growing abilities. It must be recognized that the areas of curriculum discussed in this chapter have not always been given the respect they deserve in the schools. When funding is cut, frequently the arts are eliminated. And yet, when taught well, visual and performing arts contribute greatly to the students' cognitive growth and, very importantly, their positive self-esteem. These are the areas that literally keep students in school through the rough years when they are working through the difficult phases of rapid growth and self-doubt.

Demonstrating Movement

Teaching in these areas involves demonstrating movements, whether you are teaching tennis, violin, or painting. The body must be taught the combinations of movement, sometimes connected with song, speech, or instruments, such as paintbrushes or tubas, that produce the result desired. Perfecting the art in all of these areas involves hours, even years, of practice. It is said that practice makes perfect, but that is true only if the practice is perfecting the desired movements. That is where video comes in.

Just as teachers of other subjects must begin to collect teaching videos to use in their presentations, teachers of the movement arts must do the same. A demonstration of a tennis serve by the teacher can be done only in real time. This can be enhanced somewhat by camcorders that feature still and strobe effects. The strobe serves as "pseudo-slo-mo" for many action sequences such as sports and dance. To achieve true slow motion effects, however, means having to acquire expensive editing-playback equipment.

Many sports and movement arts videos can be rented or purchased if producing an original one in the classroom proves unworkable. But even without motion, the single most important advantage that video has is shooting close-ups. Being able to show students detail—enlargement of the activity—of an active demonstration—a ballet step, the dynamics of jumping a hurdle—enables them to see and understood better.

Shooting a performance of tap dancing on stage allows the camera to become an invisible person on that stage, watching as dancers' feet are featured alone in a video frame, tilting up to catch the spiritual-like expression of a dancer's face, panning over to see the lyrical movement of a hand, tilting down to watch the orchestra conductor directing the timing and rhythm of the dancer. All of this is achieved with a single camcorder operated by a single person.

Perfecting the movement arts involves making the student very aware of the body's movement and position in space. Gradually making students more aware of exactly what their bodies are doing is the difficult part of this instruction. Videotaping this movement and then having the student view the tape help the student to see the position of the body and the movement that is taking place. This use of video heightens this awareness of movement and position in space. It also allows the student to see the progress that is taking place when videos are made on a periodic basis.

Videotaping an advanced performer and a student performer as they practice the same movements side by side gives the student a graphic comparison of movements and allows him to identify areas on which to focus.

This use of video is nothing new at the more advanced phases of training. But many students never get beyond the very basic phases of the movement arts. Because they are not given enough attention early in their school lives, they choose not to participate beyond what is required. Even by second grade, teachers begin to hear statements from students declaring, "I'm not good at P.E. [or music or drawing]!" Every child can feel good about their participation in the movement arts, but the instruction must start early, be consistent throughout the school career, and be geared toward participation, understanding, and enjoyment, not necessarily perfection. The Visual and Performing Arts Framework (California Department of Education, 1996) gives clear examples of how this continual growth is fostered. Activities for the primary grades include the following:

Dance: Students respond by moving to various stimuli: sounds, music, colors, textures, objects, imagery, and feelings.

Music: Students demonstrate perceptual skills by moving to music, answering questions about it, and describing it.

Theater: Students use their bodies to move as objects, animals, or people they have observed.

Visual Arts: Students use a variety of two- and three-dimensional media on different surfaces to communicate ideas and feelings.

All of these activities encourage the active involvement of the student while building his understanding of the media that can be used to express thoughts, feelings, and knowledge. All of the examples can also be captured on video to allow self-reflection.

Inclusion of movement activities, art, drama, and music integrated throughout the curriculum is the goal. How can students be expected to understand the history and culture of the ancient world or present-day culture without the inclusion of these disciplines?

Teaching Strategies in Physical Education and the Visual and Performing Arts

Using video to teach in the movement arts breaks down into three strategies: demonstrating movement, showing exemplary practices, and using videotapes for personal analysis and goal setting. Demonstrating movement by video allows the movement to be slowed, analyzed, and discussed. Showing exemplary practice allows the demonstration of the movement at its very best. Videotaping personal performance so that it can be viewed, analyzed, and improved is the practical application. This use of videotaping provides the encouragement that supports continued involvement on the part of the student. It is very important to note that *encouragement* is the key word. Progress has to be celebrated for the videotaping to be a positive experience.

In the beginning, many people are very reluctant to be videotaped. With the exception of young children, who enjoy watching themselves on tape, being videotaped is often not a pleasant experience. It should be evident that the answer to this dilemma is to begin the practice of videotaping early in the student's career, and then this strategy can be used throughout the school years because the students will be accustomed to the process. If the student has not had the experience of being videotaped until later in the school career, it is important to introduce videotaping in a positive manner. Discuss *how* the tape will be used ahead of time. Personal performance videos should *never* be shown to anyone publicly without the individual's consent. A good way to begin the process is to do the taping, allow the individual to take the tape home and view and analyze it privately and then view it with the instructor privately so that the self-evaluation can be compared with the evaluation of the instructor and goals set for improvement.

What types of performances should be videotaped? Periodic videotaping of performances in physical education, theater, dance, and music supports the students' knowledge of their own movements and interpretations and allows them to set personal goals.

In visual arts, the stages in the creation of a project can be captured on videotape. These videotapes can be used for student reflection and goal setting for future projects.

Exemplary performances on videotape can be used by teachers in all areas for teaching and motivating. When teaching young children in physical education and visual and performing arts, their disposition toward engaging in these activities must always be considered. Understanding the various ways of responding and expressing oneself is an important goal, as is the use of physical, visual, and performing arts as leisure and communication activities.

The physical education profession identifies three goals in teaching kindergarten through high school students: movement skills and knowledge, self-image and personal development, and social development (California Department of Education, 1994).

Within these three goal areas are listed the skill areas and content areas. The skills listed are sensorimotor and perceptual motor, locomotor, nonlocomotor, balance, eye-hand coordination, eye-foot coordination, general coordination, and creative movement. The content areas listed include rhythms and dance, aquatics, combatives, outdoor education, gymnastics and tumbling, individual and dual sports, team sports, mechanics and body movement, and effects of physical education on dynamic health.

Although this is an exhaustive list, as a classroom teacher, knowing what is desirable in a strong physical education curriculum allows you to integrate many of these goals, skills, and content areas into units of study in the classroom. Movement activities often can be easily integrated within thematic studies incorporating social sciences and the language arts. As this integration takes place, the students can be encouraged to participate in movement activities routinely. Videotaping these activities provides a way to celebrate the participation and growth in movement, along with growth seen in the more common classroom activities of social studies and language arts.

In the visual and performing arts, the students' participation over time is an important aspect of integrating these areas into their leisure and vocational goals. For students to accomplish satisfying levels of performance and continue their participation voluntarily, they must be taught skills on an ongoing basis. Teachers of these subjects must find ways for students to become familiar with a wide variety of visual and performing arts: listening to music and viewing theater, dance, and art. Video can be used to provide students opportunities to become familiar with and knowledgeable about great art, music, and theater and to spark their interest in participation.

Using Movement in Academics

Giving students opportunities to use movement to document their understanding of traditional academic studies is another way to encourage their participation in the movement arts. Showing understanding and appreciation of a book read by doing a mime or dance presentation or designing a movement game validates the student's movement knowledge and also provides an alternative way to demonstrate knowledge.

The *Visual and Performing Arts Framework* (California Department of Education, 1996) provides direction in the areas of dance, music, theater, and the visual arts. Direction provided by teachers in the areas of visual and performing arts emphasizes the importance of valuing the contribution of these curricular areas to the development of creativity, culture, and aesthetic literacy. Specialists in these teaching areas emphasize essential ideas in the arts. These essential ideas include providing opportunities for students to see the arts as core subjects that can add immeasurably to students' experiences in ways to make meaning, to evoke a wide variety of emotions, to use technology creatively, and to participate more fully in society.

In addition to the essential ideas in the visual and performing arts, the arts encompass four components: artistic perception, creative expression, historical and cultural context, and aesthetic valuing. When developed and supported over time, these components enable students to fully experience the essential ideas. The students become informed viewers and participants and understand and value the role of the arts in history and in the full enjoyment of life.

It is evident when reading the essential ideas and components of the visual and performing arts curriculum that the arts can be taught and encouraged in at least two ways: instruction and participation in the individual art forms and integration of the arts into thematic study encompassing many other curricular areas. It can also be argued that the production of video within the classroom setting falls within both categories of visual and performing arts. It is also easy to incorporate examples of physical education and the visual and performing arts within projects and thematic study within in-depth studies in language arts, science, mathematics, and the social sciences. The games, dance, art, music, and theater of the times are important to the understanding of the culture. These areas can all be taught, motivated, and documented using the video medium. Video of the best examples of the arts, taped in museums or on field trips, can be included as a part of the video teaching library.

Shooting Good Movement Video: Tips

For shooting so-called movement videos—performances and sports, for example—it is best to be thoroughly familiar with the elements of the performance or as much of the sequencing of the sports event as possible. Viewing a play or a musical before videotaping it allows the videographer to take note of all that takes place on stage with the performers and the relationship to the scenery and the props. If it is possible, it is helpful to videotape an entire performance "wide" first and then to study it carefully during playback. Using this first wide tape provides an opportunity to plan a sequence of wide, medium, and close-up shots for the next, more formal shoot. Having advance knowledge of when to zoom in and on which characters to focus improves the quality of the finished video.

The same type of planning should go into shooting a sports activity or event. Knowing the rules and key players ahead of time is a definite advantage. For track events, for example, being familiar with the schedule of events and their locations ahead of time allows you to plan where to position the camera for the best shots. For sports events, it is important to take the crowd into consideration, both for showing its excitement and for avoiding its interference during key shots. Your video will be greatly improved if you have an opportunity to view similar events prior to videotaping. If you are following a specific athlete, it is helpful to watch the person's movements and practice following the athlete with the camera.

In all movement events in which the action begins at point A and moves to point B, it is important to lead with the camera, staying just in front of the athletes. If you are shooting a baseball game, you must determine how much of the hit ball you are going to follow before you aim the camera at the runner. You cannot simply shoot a wide shot for the entire game; that would make a boring video. You will find yourself making many judgment calls in shooting sports, but they become easier to make the more familiar you are with the game, its rules, and your own experience with the camcorder. When practicing action video or teaching others to shoot action video, viewing professional sports on television is helpful. Talk about the shots, sequencing, and timing used by the television camerapersons and the effects they are able to obtain and then practice them with live action events.

Viewing and analyzing televised artistic and athletic events gives student and adult videographers a better understanding of the elements of good movement video.

Using Special Effects

Most camcorders are equipped with a high-speed shutter function that allows you to shoot scenes that include fast movement. Using the high-speed function allows you to play back the scenes on still or slow motion and maintain sharp picture and good detail. Sometimes you can enhance the movement using the strobe effect that most camcorders have as standard equipment. Keep in mind, however, that a little strobe can go a long way. There is always a danger of overdoing any video effect or movement, such as overzooming, swish-panning, and see-sawing with tilts or pans.

One important tip to remember is that once you have established the side of the sporting event you will shoot from, stick to that position. It can disorient a viewer if you shoot from one side of the football field for 10 minutes and then walk around and shoot from the other side for a while. Changing sides also causes enormous problems when you try to edit or assemble a master tape. If, for some reason, it is necessary to change sides of the football field or tennis court due to lighting problems, for example, shoot from the end of the field or court for a few minutes on the way to the other side. This helps the viewers to re-orient themselves and you when you assemble the footage so that it makes sense.

Videotaping Stage Productions

If possible, shoot a stage presentation with two cameras, one specifically for medium and close shots and the other staying wide to medium wide during the performance. This gives you a definite advantage in assembling a more professional-looking finished product than you can achieve with only one camera.

Finding a suitable location from which to shoot the stage is very important. Most stage directors want to make sure that their actors are not distracted by the camera and that the audience is always considered when placing cameras in the theater. Unless the performance is being staged specifically for videotaping, which allows much more advantageous camera placement—even on the stage itself—you will likely be shooting from the far aisles of the theater. If you are shooting with a single camcorder, it is often better to position the camera in the balcony, where your chances of shooting from a center aisle may be better.

In shooting sporting events or stage performances, consider shooting other features such as interviews with the winners, a coach, the leads in a play, or the director or quick interviews with sports fans or members of the audience. These will add a professional touch to your finished product.

USING VIDEO TO MOTIVATE IN PHYSICAL EDUCATION AND THE VISUAL AND PERFORMING ARTS

As has been discussed in previous chapters, just the act of videotaping a performance usually motivates a performer. Being aware in advance when the videotaping will take place provides motivation to prepare well. In the movement and visual arts, however, there are unique ways in which videotaping can be used to motivate.

Videotaping periodic performance reviews and comparing the more recent tape with previous tapes and with goals set earlier provide an effective way of motivating practice and goal setting. Self-evaluation of the videotape using a scoring rubric is an effective way to combine assessment and motivation. The *Physical Education Framework* (California Department of Education, 1996) includes a generic performance standard that identifies six levels of performance. See Figure 5.1 for an explanation of those levels of performance.

F I G U R E

5.1

Scoring Rubric for Physical Performance Tasks

Level	Standard of Performance by a Student to Be Achieved at a Specified Level
6	Achieves purpose of the task fully while insightfully interpreting, extending beyond the task, or raising provocative questions.
5	Accomplishes the purpose of the task.
4	Completes purpose of the task substantially.
3	Does not achieve purpose of the task fully; needs elaboration; uses some strategies perhaps ineffectually or inappropriately; makes assumptions about the purposes that are perhaps flawed.
2	Does not achieve important purposes of the task; perhaps needs redirection of work; allows completion to be affected by approach to task.
1	Does not accomplish purposes of the task.

Adapted from California Department of Education, *California Physical Education Framework.* Sacramento: Author, 1994, pp. 66–67.

Providing Expectations through the Use of Videos

Giving students careful instructions about what is expected of them in a movement or arts project and then videotaping the project for them to view and analyze their performances is an important part of teaching them to self-evaluate. Once the project is viewed on video, the students can then be asked to rate their individual performance or contribution based on a set standard. The keys to this type of assessment are the instruction given prior to the performance or project and the knowledge of the criteria to be used for judging the result.

Goal setting and periodic attention to the progress that students are making is important to keep motivation high. Portfolios have long been used in the visual arts, but they have traditionally been showcase portfolios, examples of the best works. Developmental portfolios are more motivational to the beginning-and-middle level performers. Developmental portfolios or work in progress portfolios allow the performer to view current works and compare them to work done in the past and to provide opportunities for celebration of even small growth. In art, videotaping works in progress gives the opportunity to demonstrate the sequence of techniques used and examine the work in progress at each stage. This gives the artist a history of a piece of work and allows demonstration of unique approaches. Sometimes videotaping the artist at work points out flaws in technique or areas in which improvement can be made. These videos are sometimes surprising to the artist or performer. Because some forms of art are too large and cumbersome to be shown easily, a video showing the work from many angles is often preferable to a still photograph.

In the performance arts, videos of sample performances over time are very effective in showing developing technique. A variety of performances can be videotaped to show versatility, or one standard performance can be repeated over time to show growth in technique.

USING VIDEO TO DOCUMENT AND CELEBRATE

Using video to document growing competencies in physical education and the visual and performing arts should also include some video segments that allow the students to express themselves verbally about their interests, aspirations, and goals. These video segments highlight the unique nature of the students' training and commitment and any unusual thought and goals and provides a chance for the students to reflect on the personal importance of these areas of their education.

Individual conferences in which the portfolio video is viewed and discussed provide an opportunity for the students to examine the role of physical education or the visual or performing arts in their lives. These conferences also provide an opportunity for celebration and validation of what is very often a long-term commitment to quality.

Videotaping Auditions and Applications

Performance portfolios, while motivational to some, are usually used to document and celebrate growth. They are often required by companies, colleges, and professional schools as a part of the application process. The quality of the video submitted can be a major help (or hindrance) in this application process.

Video Tips for Resume or Application Videos

1. Keep it brief. This is the main thing to keep in mind when submitting a videotape for job or professional school applications. Your tape could be among dozens submitted for the same school, job, or company, and personnel who watch them often make judgment about an applicant within the first 5 to 7 minutes, so it is important to present your information—and yourself—as quickly and thoroughly as possible.

2. Organize your tape well. In the first minute, tell the audience—on camera—your name, where you live, your educational status, your career goals, and why you are sending the application to that company or school. Mention that more detailed information is included in your cover letter.

In the next 3 to 4 minutes, include as many samples of your work as you can, introduced by you, including your exact roles in each of the samples. For example, if you helped produce your class's parent orientation tape, state that fact, and then use a 15- to 30-second segment of the video. If you were particularly proud of your science project and you did all the work yourself and kept a good video record of it, state that on camera followed by the best 30 seconds of that piece of the video, and so forth. If you are an artistic performer, include a sample of your singing or dancing. If you are outstanding in sports, or even pretty good, let your video show your skills, each time introduced by you and stating your active role in the event. When necessary, narrate what the video is showing to further explain and identify the segment.

Use the last minute to explain why you think you would be an asset to the school or company to which you are applying and remind it, once again, that more information is available in the resume and cover letter that accompany the video tape. Conclude with a polite thank you for the time and consideration given to your presentation.

3. Plan your clothing and setting. Use a simple uncluttered setting for your on-camera segments. Wear clothing that does not "shout" at the camera. Avoid solid black or all white. Take care in selecting any jewelry that might distract. Sit in front of a neutral wall. Situate a plant to one side and behind you to add a touch of dimension to the composition. Make sure your face is lit fully from the key light stand position (at an angle from the front). Position a stand lamp to give you backlight, separating you from the wall.

4. Frame the video. Have the camera operator shoot you in a medium close-up—framing head and shoulders. Look directly into the camera, be serious, but smile. If no camera operator is available, you may have to videotape the presentation yourself. Sit in the position you will use.

    a. Sit up straight and place a yardstick on top of your head and let the end of it rest on the wall behind you. Holding the yardstick firmly with one hand, lightly mark the wall with a piece of masking tape to show where the top of your head will be in the shot.

    b. From behind the camera (on a tripod), zoom into the piece of tape on the wall, which now represents the top of your head. Focus on the tape and adjust the camera so it is in your viewfinder but has some headroom above it.

    c. Start the camera, walk into the frame from behind the camera, sit down, and begin your narrative. When you are seated, your head and body should cover the piece of tape on the wall. You may want to practice this a time or two to make sure your framing is accurate.

5. Retape until you're satisfied. Record all of your on-camera segments from start to finish, pausing for at least 8 to 10 seconds between each of your narratives. If you make a mistake, identify the segment, followed by a numerical reference to the take or attempt on video. For example, if you made an error or had to clear your throat on the second of your narrative segments, pause, and then state on camera, "segment 2, take 2," which identifies the narrative and the second attempt at getting a complete segment. Continue to tape until you have several attempts for each segment and you feel that you have a good take on each segment.

6. Assemble your videotape. When assembling your resume or performance portfolio tape, you need two VCR playback/record machines, one for playback of all previously recorded material and the second for your master tape recording. If a second VCR is not available, you may use the camcorder as a playback unit instead of the VCR. Refer to the operator's manuals for proper cable connections.

Determine the video segments you want to use from your portfolio tape and make a log of the portions of those segments you intend to include on your master tape. Do the same for your on-camera segments, choosing the best ones, of course. If you plan to use graphics, camera cards, illustrations, and so on you can prerecord those on a separate videotape so you can select from them as you assemble the master.

If you use a graphic title—The Video Resume of Mary Smith, for example—it will be the first segment you dub from the playback VCR to the master VCR. Start the VCR with *play/record* and let it roll about 10 seconds and then push *play* on the playback VCR. An appropriate length for this title—an uncomplicated one—is about 6 to 7 seconds or the time it takes to read it aloud slowly. If you recorded the graphic with black on either end, the timing should be slightly longer.

Pause the VCR on which you are assembling the master tape. Find your next segment, probably the first of your on-camera narration where you introduce yourself. Position the playback segment about 2 seconds before you actually begin to speak and push *play* on the playback and *record* on the record machine simultaneously and allow that segment to record, leaving about 5 additional seconds past the point where you actually finish your narrative. Repeat the procedure until you have assembled all desired segments on your master tape.

After the final segment has been recorded, pause the tape once again, find a segment of black on your playback tape, and record it at the end of the last image on your master. You have completed your tape. Make certain that both the videotape master and its box container are accurately labeled.

USING VIDEO TO INVOLVE PARENTS

Including parents in the viewing and celebration of portfolio videos in physical education and the visual and performing arts is effective in helping them see the goals of the programs and the progress the students are making. It allows the parents to see the students' levels of accomplishment, compare the present and past levels of performance, and be involved in the discussion of the students' interests and aspirations. These opportunities also provide the teachers with a chance to explain the goals and objectives of the curriculum and the advantages of study in these areas. As was noted early in this chapter, physical education and the visual and performing arts are often viewed as "frills" by some parents. Portfolio conferences with parents gives the teachers a way to communicate the important benefits of physical fitness, athletic and artistic literacy, and accomplishments. There are also many ways in which videos available to parents would support their understanding of their role in encouraging their children's participation and pursuit of excellence in physical education and the visual and performing arts. Some suggested titles follow:

> Field Trips for Parents and Children: Encouraging Interest in Physical Education and the Visual and Performing Arts
> Ballanchine to Wagner: Basic Artistic Literacy for Families
> A Trip to the Art Museum: How to Prepare Your Child
> A Trip to the Ballet: How to Prepare Your Child
> A Trip to the Opera: How to Prepare Your Child
> Taking Your Child to Athletic Events: How to Prepare and Involve Her

Because the videotaping of active endeavors is sometimes challenging, choose a physical education, dance, or movement activity that you would like to document. Plan the shoot by writing a basic script explaining the activity, planning a storyboard, and practicing some active video shots before making the video. Choose an activity that will be interesting to your students and can be used for instruction or celebration in your class.

PRACTICE ACTIVITY

Evaluating and Improving Your Video

As you view your video practice activity, use the rubric in Figure 5.2 to evaluate the quality of the video. When you plan your video project for this chapter, use what you have learned from the practice exercise to make the video project more professional. Be sure to choose a project that you will be able to add to your video teaching library.

Video Project

Select a video project in physical education or the visual or performing arts that will be a valuable addition to your video teaching library. Some suggestions follow:

A demonstration of an active technique that you can use to demonstrate something you want to teach.

F I G U R E   *Rubric for Evaluating Action Videos*

5.2

Continuity

| Action jumps around. | Action is sometimes hard to follow. | Action can be followed with few exceptions. | Action flows well. | Action is easy to follow, viewer does not notice scene changes. |

Framing

| Camera framing is poor (people move out of shots). | Camera framing is often off. | Camera framing does not detract. | Camera framing enhances the shots. | Camera framing is excellent. |

Focus

Poor< – >Excellent

Sequence

Poor< – >Excellent

Narration

Poor< – >Excellent

A video of an active, culminating activity that you can use to demonstrate your expectations to future classes.

A video of a special event that you can use to celebrate the accomplishments of your class (Olympic Day, a play performance, etc.)

Use all the techniques you have learned so far to make the video as professional and enjoyable as possible. Remember to plan thoroughly, write a script, prepare a storyboard, and actively involve your students.

SUMMARY

Using video to teach in the movement arts breaks down into three strategies: demonstrating movement, showing exemplary practices, and videotaping activities for personal analysis and goal setting. Using video to accomplish these three aspects of teaching enhances the instruction and the involvement of the students in physical education and the visual and performing arts.

Integration of games, dance, art, music, and theater into units of study in the social sciences and literature encourages students to develop a deeper understanding of the history and culture of different peoples and times. Videotaping the students' active involvement allows them to view their performance and to set goals for themselves and then to evaluate their progress.

The use of video to document students' growth over time is an important motivation. Although not all students will accomplish the same levels of accomplishment in physical education and the visual and performing arts, an important goal in these curricular areas is an appreciation of the beauty that can be created in various art and movement forms. A basic level of competence in all the movement and visual arts is an important part of developing a well-rounded individual. For this goal to be met, ongoing instruction, participation, and encouragement are necessary.

The use of video to build individual portfolios is an important aspect of documenting and celebrating the students' involvement. In the case of students who have aspirations to continue their education or employment in the movement or visual arts, this portfolio serves an important role in gaining entrance to higher levels of training.

Two types of video libraries will increase the effectiveness of teaching. The teacher's library of video used in instruction is vital to being able to demonstrate movement, give students access to the masters of the art being studied, and demonstrate expectations in assignments. Using parents' lending libraries of videotapes encourages parents to become active supporters of the goals of physical education, visual, and performing arts. Parents are also a part of the team in gathering video that is used in the classroom. Family trip and cultural event videos can be easily copied and added to the video teaching library.

In all these endeavors, student participation in the planning and production of video encourages their use of special talents and interests such as writing, videography, editing, and directing.

REFERENCES

California Department of Education. (1994). *Physical Education Framework*. Sacramento, CA: California Department of Education.

California Department of Education. (1996). *Visual and Performing Arts Framework*. Sacramento, CA: California Department of Education.

SUGGESTED READINGS

Berg, B., and Turner, D. 1993. MTV unleashed: Sixth graders create music videos based on works of art. *Tech Trends, 38* (3), 28–31.

Bledsoe, P. M. (1992). Performance and Evaluation of Communicative Tasks: The Video Camera in the K-2 Classroom. *Hispania, 75.*

Brown, K. 1993. Video production in the classroom: Creating success for students and schools. *Tech Trends, 38* (3), 32-35.

Carucio, S. (March/April, 1991). Facilitating a student-produced video. *Media Methods,* 26–27, 54–55.

Dickson, C. (1990). Lights. . .camera. . .action! *Training and Development Journal,* 44(10), 49–52.

Gardner, H. (1993) *Multiple Intelligences: The Theory in Practice.* New York: Basic Books.

Hargis, M. (May/June, 1990). The video yearbook. *Media and Methods,* 20–21.

Kilianek, K. (1995). Using still video and digital cameras to motivate students. *Media and Methods, 32* (1), 10–12.

Peters, R. E. 1989. Enhancing curricula with film and video. *Media and Methods*, *26* (2), 30.

6

Using Video for Schoolwide and Long-Term Projects

The Way We Were

Mrs. Medders is greeting the kindergartners as they enter the room on the first day of the school year. As they come into the room, she asks their names and helps them to find their name tags. Her video helper from the sixth grade is getting all these interactions on tape. As the first morning progresses, the children are videotaped as they learn to find their storage cubbies and wash their hands for a snack, even as they cry for their moms.

Periodically throughout the year, videos are made to document their activities: field trips, school parties, plays, and special events. The children enjoy watching themselves on television, and the parents enjoy viewing their children participating in kindergarten, but Mrs. Medders has a secret. The videotape is put away in the principal's office at the end of the school year. It is carefully marked "Kindergarten 1996–97" and kept to be shown at the students' sixth grade graduation party.

At the end of each year, the sixth graders, feeling very full of themselves as they get ready to move to the middle school, view themselves as they were in that first year of school. They find the videos hilarious as they see how much they've grown and learned over their elementary school years. As the sixth graders leave their party, each of them receives a copy of this precious memory of their kindergarten year.

Mr. Suga, the principal, beams as the parents thank him for this marvelous surprise. His response is the same every year, "Kindergarten is the most precious memory. I'm so glad Mrs. Medders thought of this special project."

Washington High School seniors are gathered around the VCR in the media center viewing their video classbook. "This is so neat!" exclaims Suzanne as scenes from the Homecoming Dance are shown. "It's so much more exciting than the photos in the printed classbook!"

"I missed seeing my brother's touchdown in the Lincoln game," says Bonnie as scenes from the football game are shown. "I was in bed with the flu. My dad's going to be so proud of this video!"

The video classbook is a wonderful addition to the traditional printed classbook. Many schools across the country are beginning to produce these active classbooks either as an addendum to the traditional classbook or as a student-produced product. A video classbook allows the students to relive the excitement of the big game, the beauty of everyone dressed up and dancing to the popular music of the year at the school dances, and the special events that are such a special part of a high school senior year. The plays, debates, and fundraisers all come to life on a video classbook.

Training video helpers provides a school cadre of videographers to support taping in many classrooms.

CHAPTER OBJECTIVES

As you can see from these brief vignettes, video can serve to provide a lasting memory of special times and projects in the lives of children and young adults. The goal of this chapter is to introduce a variety of schoolwide or long-term projects that support the learning environment and involve parents as a part of the instructional team. After reading this chapter and completing the video practice activity, you will learn:

1. To understand ways to use videos to integrate curriculum, document units of study, and celebrate special events and projects.
2. To use videos to improve school-parent-community public relations.
3. To use videos to improve student learning.
4. To use videos for teacher education, student orientations, and parent involvement.
5. To learn techniques for creating video classbooks.
6. To use videos to create time capsules.
7. To learn how to store and protect videotapes.

8. To learn ways to set up a video club to provide technical assistance for producing quality video products throughout the curriculum.
9. To understand how to plan for the gradual addition of video equipment as needed.
10. To learn ways to use video in teacher reflection and evaluation.

USING VIDEO TO INTEGRATE CURRICULUM PROJECTS

As has been noted previously, any video project is, by definition, an integrated project. To produce a quality video, a script must be written, a storyboard produced, and a sequence of video shots must be planned and timed. These are technical and artistic elements, and collaboration is necessary. Using the medium of video to produce a culminating activity for an integrated unit of study allows the accomplishments of the students to be documented and celebrated and even evaluated. The integration of writing, art, music, physical movements, speech, and drama becomes a part of a well-planned video project. Some suggestions for innovative approaches to integrated culminating projects include these:

A reader's theater production written and performed by the students, bringing together all the information learned in a thematic study.

An opera written and performed by the students, including elements of art, music, and dance. The opera includes information gained from a unit of study: *Tommy Tooth* in first grade, *Pilgrim's Progress* in third grade, *Life in Ancient Egypt* in sixth grade, *The Melting Pot Becomes the Salad Bowl* in junior high, and *A Modern-Day Julius Caesar* in high school.

A simulation trip or reenactment of history after a study of a certain period of history, including samples of the art, crafts, music, dance, and games of the country or time being studied.

A neighborhood improvement project showing before and after scenes as well as a history of the project, documenting the collaboration accomplished.

All of these integrated projects require planning, collaboration, and time. The students gain valuable experience in thinking through all aspects of the project, including planning and implementation. Even if the teacher has a well-conceived idea of the final project in the very beginning, involving the students in brainstorming, setting priorities, gathering props and supplies, writing the script, and making the storyboards are worthwhile learning activities in themselves. The most exciting day comes at the culmination of all this, the viewing of the finished project! The best part of a video project is that all the students can have a copy to take home.

Another technique for culminating projects is making a video animated cartoon. This involves students in writing and illustrating a script that can be based in any curriculum area. Professional video animation is an elaborate process, involving equipment that includes computers, laser discs, and other expensive, professional paraphernalia. A form of animation can be accomplished with camcorders that have the interval recording, or time-lapse, feature as discussed in Chapter 3.

Many camcorders also include a frame-by-frame advance feature that allows you to manually (or even automatically with some models) shoot objects such as clay figures or drawings, one or more frames at a time, moving or changing their positions of the objects a little each shooting interval until the desired action sequence has been accomplished. In the case of illustrated cartoons, the pages are photographed in sequence to complete the filming of a cartoon similar to the old "flip-book cartoons."

As with shooting time-lapse sequences, the camera, tripod, and the object in the frame must remain in the same location and perspective, or the result will not be effective. The process is very time-consuming and generally results in only a few seconds of actual tape playback time. While this will not render the "slick" professional movement that we're accustomed to seeing on commercial TV ads, the students generally see the process as a challenge and enjoy doing it. This project is especially effective if one or more of the students is a good cartoonist, and, it allows a variation in the presentation of culminating activities.

USING VIDEOS TO IMPROVE SCHOOL-PARENT-COMMUNITY PUBLIC RELATIONS

Video productions that show the goals of the school, ways that parents and community can become involved, and celebrations of community-based projects are helpful in cementing community relations. Helping parents to understand why projects are undertaken and ways that they can become more involved with them can have valuable outcomes. Used at PTA meetings and parent conferences, the videos help the parents to understand that their participation is encouraged and valued. The videos, when shown to community service organizations, often encourage their participation in school projects. Some suggested projects include the following:

Parent and community resource volunteers. Bringing parents and community people into schools to share special talents such as painting or sculpture, playing musical instruments, quilting, or interests such as astronomy, rocket building, woodworking, and cooking.

School beautification. Bringing parents and volunteers into the schools to work with the students in planning and implementing projects such as gardening (vegetable or flowers and shrubs), painting and refurbishing, sign painting, mural painting, and other special decorating projects.

Neighborhood safety. Bringing police and fire safety officials to classes to meet with students, parents, and neighborhood volunteers plan ways to make the neighborhood safer. Many schools have also involved neighborhood safety committees in planning a safe Halloween celebration for the children and families in the neighborhood.

Multicultural committee. Bringing members of all the ethnic and cultural groups in the neighborhood to classes to plan and celebrate food festivals, music and dance festivals, and special holidays and to participate in "getting-to-know-you" activities. Their involvement helps to foster multicultural awareness and acceptance.

USING VIDEOS TO IMPROVE STUDENT LEARNING

As has been noted in each of the previous chapters, videos made to help parents to understand ways in which they can support their children's learning are very effective in building home-school communication. In addition, videos that directly support student and parent learning are valuable. From the beginning of a child's school career, making storybook videos available for home use supports early literacy development in the child. If the parents or older students in the home are illiterate or marginally literate, watching the storybook videos together provides opportunities for family literacy. These storybook videos must focus on the text, of course, if this is to take place. Storybook videos also demonstrate effective interaction strategies for storybook reading. Several studies have demonstrated that it is not just the reading of the text but also the verbal interactions focused on the illustrations, text, and related experiences that foster interest and proficiency in reading aloud (Sulzby, 1991; Lamme, 1988).

At each step of the child's school career, there are techniques for study that, demonstrated and made available on videotape, can be viewed at home by children and their parents to support habits that foster good scholarship.

Many parents do not realize the importance of such mundane interactions as dinner table conversations, discussion of news and entertainment shows on television, or discussions of television commercials. The learning that takes place in the family setting when parents make the most of these opportunities for learning and bonding makes the sharing of this information via home-school videos a valuable endeavor.

When vital lessons are taught in the classroom and a student is absent, videotaping the lesson for the student to view at a later time saves the teacher valuable time. If lessons are generally difficult for students to grasp, videotaping them provides two unique opportunities. First, the teacher has a chance to view and evaluate the lesson. Perhaps changes can be made to make the explanation more understandable. Second, students have the chance to watch the explanation and demonstration a second, third, or more times.

Uses for videotaped instruction in your classroom
- A number of students are absent and may need to view the tape to catch up with the class.
- When you are teaching a difficult concept that may require additional review by individual students.
- When you are assigning a long-range project, especially when it will require parental support.
- When a substitute teacher might use the lesson in the future.

For long-range projects, a videotape that explains the process and expectations is valuable, both to the student and the parents. If possible, a timeline, which breaks the long-range project into achievable pieces, helps the students to stay on schedule. Instructions on how the project is to be submitted, or displayed saves valuable time and frustration.

Some of these videos are best made available from the teachers at the school. Others are best housed in the school media center or parent resource center. If your school does not have a parent resource center, take-home videos may be a way to start one.

USING VIDEOS FOR TEACHER EDUCATION, STUDENT ORIENTATIONS, AND PARENT INVOLVEMENT

If your school is spending valuable funds bringing in curriculum or classroom management consultants, always ask if they mind being videotaped. Many of them will agree to this, providing a valuable resource for review at a later date or for viewing by absent teachers or new teachers hired. Often, a few weeks or months down the line, viewing the videotape and following it with a discussion of the implementation process is extremely valuable.

Basic orientation videos for incoming students, new teachers, and parent groups serve to communicate the rules, expectations, and opportunities for involvement. Videos available in multiple languages are very helpful for parents who would normally need a translator. Videos that explain the immunizations and physical examinations required for school entrance are useful for parent orientations or late-entering students. Making these available in multiple languages is vital in certain areas of the country.

Another innovation that is proving helpful in schools and businesses across the nation is the use of a "video loop" that provides information to visitors in the building. A *video loop* is a videotape on which information about scheduled events is shared, usually in graphics format, although video clips can be included. The video clip/information notice is recorded over and over, back-to-back on a 2-hour tape as many times as it will fit on the tape. A visitor entering the office or school can stand briefly and view the video loop to get information about all the scheduled events for the day or week and then proceed. Video loops can be played on a VCR/monitor combination that can be programmed to run to the end of the tape, automatically rewind, and begin again. (Egan, 1996).

CREATING VIDEO YEARBOOKS AND CLASSBOOKS

Gerald Millerson, in *Video Production Handbook,* 2nd edition, may not have had video yearbooks in mind when he wrote the following, but much of what he says is vital to such a project:

> You cannot just point a camera at a scene and expect it to convey all the information and atmosphere that the. . . cameraman is experiencing. A camera is inherently selective. It can only show certain limited aspects of a situation at any time. (156)

That pretty well sums up what producing a video yearbook entails. You cannot "just point a camera at a scene" until you know—well in advance—what the camera is supposed to include. And you cannot decide in advance what those elements will be until they have been discussed by all the essential personnel—in this case, administrators, teachers, and students—and put in writing, which is to say, scripted. So it's back to preproduction in its most encompassing form.

One of the fundamental decisions that must be made when determining whether or not to produce a video yearbook is to identify what kind of basic editing equipment you will purchase because the scope of a schoolwide classbook demands that postproduction editing be an integral element in the production planning. Planning is definitely the operative word here. A yearbook scheduling plan is an important asset in keeping the shooting schedule under control. See Figure 6.1.

There is enough involved in producing a yearbook on video that it would be helpful if a part of the school year—the last semester, perhaps—is devoted solely to preproduction. Since most schools deal with schedules well in advance, there should be enough advance information as to what events are going to take place and when so that at the earliest part of the following

F I G U R E

6.1

*Sample
Video
Yearbook
Scheduling
Plan*

Month/Yearbook Video Schedule

Date	Morning	Midday	Afternoon	Evening
1	Event Crew Equipment	Event Crew Equipment	Event Crew Equipment	Event Crew Equipment
2	Event Crew Equipment	Event Crew Equipment	Event Crew Equipment	Event Crew Equipment
3	Event Crew Equipment	Event Crew Equipment	Event Crew Equipment	Event Crew Equipment
4	Event Crew Equipment	Event Crew Equipment	Event Crew Equipment	Event Crew Equipment
5	Event Crew Equipment	Event Crew Equipment	Event Crew Equipment	Event Crew Equipment

school year, all the time could be devoted to actual production and postproduction. "Doughnut holes," reserved spaces in previously edited video, could be left open for events taking place late in the school year, but eventually in the timeline, postproduction—editing, audio sweetening (see the Glossary) and distributing—must take over with its own priorities.

Production of a video classbook should include help from school personnel and students who are accustomed to such planning, such as those who work on the school paper or newsletter. Their organizational skills should prove invaluable.

Among the first decisions to be made concerns *what* events and activities are going to be included. One of the most agonizing decisions in any early planning are those about what *not* to include, but decide you must.

Perhaps the most sensitive decisions are those that involve people. Who will be represented? What are the criteria? What specific roles will these people assume?

Students might find themselves dealing with elements of a civics course in planning the video if, for example, they were called upon to vote on a "slate" of people to be included and events to be covered: sports, the debate team, coverage of social organizations, and favorite teachers; the list goes on. Keep in mind that a classbook is primarily a student project, so students must be given opportunities to have an active role in its production and final form. Rather than using a random ballot to select names and to determine issues, however, planning and organization present a manageable list of criteria to be decided by a schoolwide vote.

All categories of classbook coverage should include a student production team *and* a faculty adviser. Uniform policies must be established, so it becomes a matter of scheduling times to shoot, reserving alternate times for unexpected natural happenings such as bad weather, illness, or some other manifestation of Murphy's law.

Every student group's area of responsibility must be clearly delineated. One of the things that video classbook production cannot tolerate is a duplication of effort. The videographer assigned to the sports team must resist the effort to shoot outside the track, for example, because of the possibility of missing some activity that is his primary responsibility. The same applies to trying to squeeze two interviews in a time frame allotted to one. One of them inevitably is going to suffer. Avoiding these pitfalls is the reason for preproduction planning.

A video classbook is at least a year-long project, possibly even a multiyear project when it becomes a class video, focusing on the four years a class spends in school. It takes much planning and coordination to ensure video clips of all the major events are made over the years. Student videographers must be available to capture the most important events during the year, and a master plan for the video must be made so it is not too long. The final project becomes more like a montage of the senior year for yearbooks or four years for classbooks with a running commentary in most cases. Formats are limited only by the imagination.

If video classbooks become ongoing projects and represent the highlights of the four years in high school, certain main events of each year must be captured and used in more than one classbook. The video made at each of these events features the members of the class in whose video classbook it will be featured. This necessitates careful planning and often entails the use of videographers representing each class and taping the members of that class as they are involved in the events being filmed.

When making a yearbook or classbook video, it is important to remember that it will be viewed many times over a period of years. Including the popular music of the day and focusing on the fashions and hairstyles of the year help to preserve the atmosphere and environment of the times. If there are major news happenings, include them in the video to help put the events of the school year or years into a historical setting. Writing a script that helps bring all these elements together is not an easy task but makes the video one to be saved and savored.

Postproduction work on a yearbook or classbook video involves recapturing the sequence and pace of the period of time being memorialized. The script must be written, video segments selected and timed, and music selected to reflect the mood and the popular music of the time. With video yearbooks and classbooks, most of the video has already been filmed, and postproduction involves pulling it together in a cohesive way, but even as the video is being edited, some additional shots may be needed. Scenes at graduation and baccalaureate cannot be omitted and must be shot at the very end of the year. Don't forget to plan for end-of-the-year scenes and include them in the script.

The most effective editing for video yearbooks and classbooks involves using music and voice-over to summarize the events as video clips are shown to capture the visual image. Many video projects produced in and out of the classroom include natural sound and/or voices from on-camera presentation. The built-in microphone in the camcorder is usually adequate for most shooting situations. However, at times an auxiliary, or external, microphone will be helpful if not essential. One-on-one interviews and talk and panel programs are examples of the uses of an outside microphone. When an auxiliary microphone is plugged into the jack on the camcorder, that mike becomes the primary sound source and bypasses the camera's microphone.

Sometimes audio can be "mixed" while actually shooting the video. For example, if an announcer is describing an event while it is taking place and she is using an external microphone, the mike will pick up not only the announcer's voice but also some ambient, or natural, sound present in the shooting environment. Ambient sound can often be an unwanted distraction, so placement of the external microphone either close to the narrator or away from the ambient sound—or both—is important.

Some camcorders are equipped with an audio dub feature that allows new sound to replace audio that has been previously recorded directly onto the videotape in the camera. You can preset the portions on the tape that you want to dub over so you do not inadvertently record over portions that you want to leave intact.

Voice-overs—narration of audio over previously recorded video—are generally spoken off-camera and are usually done as a postproduction function using a VCR. This is normally done as the narrator watches video on a monitor and reads from a prepared script or ad-libs the narrative. All new model VCRs have the audio-dub feature that keeps the video portion intact while recording new audio over the old sound. It is generally a good idea for the narrator to practice timing the narrative as she watches the video before actually recording the voice-over onto the videotape.

Adding music and a voice-over is best accomplished using an audio mixer that is connected to the VCR. A mixer allows a number of audio sources to be fed into it and they, in turn, are distributed to a single audio channel of the videotape in the VCR, again without disturbing the previously recorded video. For example, if you are narrating a voice-over, you should use a lavaliere microphone because it would give you the best quality sound nearest your voice. Plug the microphone into an input source in the sound mixer and, perhaps, use an output cord from a CD playback machine for music, plugging it into another input source on the mixer. Using headsets, you could monitor the volume controls on both audio sources using the mixing board fader bars so the music does not overpower the narration but allows you to fade up the music during narrative gaps for a professional effect.

If you do not have access to a mixer, use a music source (your stereo system speakers, for example) near the microphone where you will be narrating the voice-overs. Make adjustments to ensure that your voice is the predominant sound source and that the music is heard but stays in the background. Experiment with this type of "mixing" before you commit to the actual recording.

Remember that any type of voice-over environment should be as "clean" as possible with no unwanted or extraneous sounds to interfere with the audio result that you are trying to achieve.

Although it is not likely that video yearbooks or classbooks will take the place of the traditional classbook, they certainly add an interesting visual summary of the high school, middle school, or elementary school years and are destined to be popular at class reunions.

CREATING VIDEO TIME CAPSULES

As the opening vignette in this chapter demonstrated, video time capsules are very effective ways to look back in time. Kindergarten video, saved and shown as the students move into the middle or junior high school, is not only entertaining but also provides an opportunity to celebrate growth and accomplishment.

High school video, saved for the tenth high school reunion (or even longer!) provides a wonderful chance to renew old friendships and reminisce.

The following are other video time capsule ideas:

- The news of the day discussed or the newest inventions demonstrated and saved on video at any grade, can be viewed and discussed by future classes in years to come in light of more recent happenings and inventions.
- A video production of the curriculum and study approaches in any given year, planned and videotaped by the students, provides an opportunity for them to look back at themselves at a later date or for the teacher to use the video with future classes to show the contrasts between past and current curricula and discuss practical elements of history.
- A video of the school, faculty, and staff with short clips about their personal interests and talents provides an interesting look back at the history of the school and personnel at a 10-year celebration or future reunions of students.

STORING AND PROTECTING VIDEOTAPES

Planning and using video time capsules assumes that the videotapes you make and save will last for many years. For this to happen, some thought must be given to the storage and protection of the tapes.

To begin, it is highly recommended that you purchase the best quality videocassette possible to ensure a longer life for the tape. When using a new videotape, it is a good idea to fast-forward the tape to the end and rewind it to the beginning. This is best done in a VCR machine rather than in the camcorder. This allows the tape to tighten on its reel and helps prevent the possibility of a "window," a section of tape that overlaps itself.

To get the longest life from videotapes, it is important to protect them from dust, oil from hands, humidity, extremes in temperature, and magnetic fields. To avoid these dangers, the tapes should be stored in their protective envelope with only the label end exposed. Avoid storing the tape near any strong magnetic fields such as television sets and loudspeakers. Avoid touching the videotape with your hands. Do not cut or splice videotape because this can damage the recording as well as the video heads of the VCR.

Additional precautions include keeping the tapes in their covers when not in use to protect them from dust, not leaving tapes in the VCR for long periods of time, and storing them on their narrow edges rather than flat, which keeps them from sagging and being damaged (Valmont, 1996).

RECRUITING AND TRAINING STUDENT HELP FOR VIDEO CLUBS

When video is used throughout the school, a video club is a valuable resource for the teachers. In the beginning, it is wise for interested teachers to recruit volunteers and involve them in video projects in their own classrooms. Teachers who see the value of using video in the classroom and share their enthusiasm with students are the best choices as sponsors of the video club.

Trained student videographers are a valuable asset to teachers throughout the school. Being able to provide this type of assistance to teachers gives students an important way to contribute to the school community.

Once a small group of interested students and teachers are identified, planning and implementing video projects in the classrooms create opportunities for practice in all aspects of video production. Upper grade video projects done in the classroom often provide a group of students who then help with video projects in the lower grades.

Video practice, such as those in the activities provided in this text, gives students and teachers practice in developing and perfecting their video techniques. An after-school club is a great way to provide extra time for practice as well as planning to assist in schoolwide projects. Often students have access to family-owned camcorders so that more students will have a chance to practice their video skills.

Once a cadre of trained videographers is available to assist teachers in producing classroom video projects, a teacher inservice provides the faculty with ideas for ways to include video projects in the curriculum. At this point, a scheduling system for requesting the help of the video club members must be set up.

Because of the artistic, writing, and planning skills acquired in the production of video, secondary schools can easily justify offering video production as an elective class. Having videographers available each period of the school day is a powerful way to support making classroom and schoolwide videos.

CREATING SCHOOL TELEVISION STATIONS

As schoolwide transmission of video has become more available across the nation, a series of school television stations has appeared. Many of the schools that have this transmission capability are using the schoolwide video as a unique way to motivate the writing and production of student-produced newscasts, educational programming, and special events.

At Balderas Elementary School in Fresno, California, teacher Diane Leonard wrote a grant proposal to buy the production equipment needed to produce and transmit schoolwide programming. Awarded $24,000 in 1992, Balderas was able to purchase one S-VHS camcorder, 4 VHS camcorders, an audio mixer, a title maker, a CD "boom box," a copyright-free music library, four tripods, a lighting kit, four monitors, an equipment cart, a teleprompter, and a computer. Ms. Leonard and her fifth and sixth graders produce a daily newscast that they videotape each afternoon and broadcast schoolwide each morning.

Other schools have begun with one camcorder and a VCR on a rolling cart that is moved from classroom to classroom so the students have the opportunity to view the news.

There are many opportunities to expand the television station within the school setting. Coaxial cable installed throughout the school and television monitors in each classroom enable the transmission of the programming across the entire campus. Cable companies have several services available to school television stations. TCI has a service, X-PRESS XChange, which allows schools to receive wire service news over cable lines and a converter-equipped computer. Support from cable companies varies widely. Contact your local cable company for information about what is available in your area.

One of the most popular video program formats for a school television station is the newscast. Most schools begin by producing a school-based news show and expand from there. CNN has a program that allows schools to become CNN Schools and receive permission to include CNN news segments into their local broadcasts.

A field trip to a local television station is a natural beginning for creating interest and gathering information in the production of television shows. Starting small, with a 5-minute news show several times a week and gradually moving to a daily show that can be expanded as necessary is wise. The students learn the planning and production skills needed with practice. Involving as many students as possible in writing news stories, studying other news shows, and learning camera techniques, captioning, and editing encourages the discovery and practice of unique skills. Producing a news program provides opportunities to involve a number of students in a variety of production jobs including senior producer, director, switcher, audio engineer, graphics operator, and videotape operator—all positions traditionally part of the *control room*. In the studio there are camera operators (or "ops"), a floor manager, an audio boom operator, a lighting director, and of course, the talent: the anchors, sports, and weather folks. Taking turns with the on-camera jobs gives a variety of students a chance to practice their oral presentation skills. Writers, script coordinators, and the indispensable "gofers" are equally important.

Just as producing a video classbook requires input from many sources, so does the newscast, but its result is more immediate since old news is no longer news.

The process for gathering and reporting the news involves some real-life experience in coordination. Reporters and camera people are assigned by the senior producer/assignment editor (working with the faculty adviser) to various areas of the school: classes, athletics, and the cafeteria. Each area has an assigned contact person so that "fast-breaking news" or even slow-breaking news can be included from all areas of the school. Reporters and videographers are sent out to the various areas of the school and even into the community to gather news, information, and videotape. Once ideas for stories are gathered, the reporters and camera operators meet to write the final story and edit the video. In the beginning, this usually just involves only selecting a short clip to be shown on the newscast while the anchor reads the description of what is happening on tape. With practice, the reporters soon learn to tape interviews and action footage. Each story is put on a separate videotape and carefully and accurately labeled along with a copy of the finished story.

Of course, any late-breaking stories and events must be covered. Sometimes the addition of this kind of story means that another story must be bumped. That is the nature of a newscast.

Another team can be used to shoot public service announcements (PSAs) to use during the newscast. The production of these spots takes time and should be scheduled early in the process. They can then be used periodically throughout the newscast in the place of commercials. Announcements of upcoming events, athletic schedules, dances, and deadlines all serve to make the newscast more like the real news.

After all the stories have been written and the video edited, the script coordinator and the senior producer get together to make up the rundown sheet, the master list of each element of the newscast from the opening to the "slug line" (brief description of the story), story length, whether it is a report with videotape or a read, its running time, notation of any graphics, and who will read the story. The rundown also includes placement of the PSAs or other inserts and, of course, the close and fade to black.

The script person makes copies of the script and rundown sheet for the senior editor, the director, audio engineer, tape operator, graphics operator, floor manager, and the anchors, and sports and weather persons.

The director at this point takes command of the control room and studio. The director's word is absolute for the duration of the program and his words must be within earshot of all essential personnel.

"Roll opening video. . .5. . .4. . .3. . .2. . .1. . . Opening audio up. . .Take VCR 1. . .bring down audio . . .get ready to mike and cue talent. . .Mike and cue talent. . .fade out opening audio."

You're into the show. It now becomes a matter of the director calling the shots from the script, which has been marked for easy reference to stories, talent, VCR stories, audio, and so on. Many times the director color codes each element for better reference. Everything moves very quickly during a newscast.

During the newscast the VCR tape operator has a very important job, shuttling tape stories between two videotape machines and making sure that they are cued to a 5-second roll, which the director takes into account. As soon as a tape is finished playing, it is ejected and the next one put in place and cued.

"Get ready for the close. Roll closing video. . .5. . .4. . .3 . . .2 . . . 1. . Bring up closing audio . . .Take VCR 2. . sneak in. . .audio. . .Kill anchor mikes. . .bring up music to time. . .Fade to black. That's a wrap. Thanks, everybody."

The hand signals used in producing a newscast are very important, and the students love using them. See Figure 6.2 for examples of the hand signals the students will need to learn.

When you have developed and honed your school newscast to a point at which everything and everybody seems to work as the proverbial well-oiled machine, you may want to take your show on the road, and contact the local cable station and produce some or all of your newscasts there as public access programming. Your

F I G U R E   *Hand Signals for Video Production*

6.2

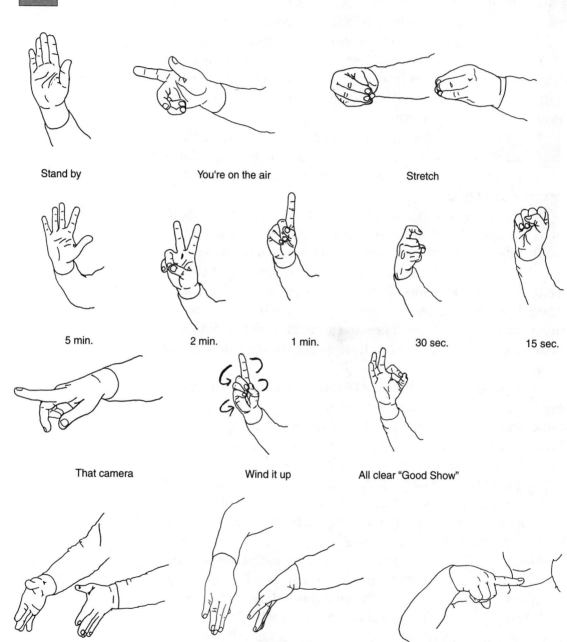

Stand by

You're on the air

Stretch

5 min.

2 min.

1 min.

30 sec.

15 sec.

That camera

Wind it up

All clear "Good Show"

Move closer together

Move apart

Cut!

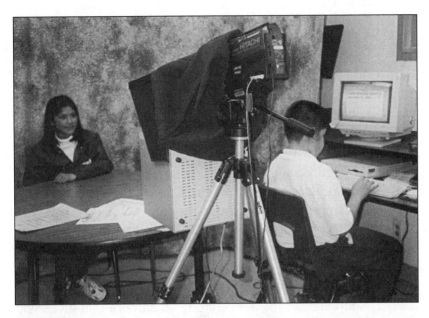

Students learn a variety of video skills through the operation of a school news station.

students will not only have an opportunity to visit a professional operation, produce with some professionals, and learn about cable operations but also have an actual audience that watches this type of cable programming on a regular basis.

ADDING TO YOUR VIDEO EQUIPMENT

In Chapter 1, we talked about the basic equipment needed to start your school and classroom video projects. As you become more familiar with both the technical and aesthetic experience of video and branch out into long-range projects such as newscasts and video classbooks, you will want to expand your equipment inventory.

If you began with just one camera, your next purchase should include at least one, preferably two, more camcorders, upgraded, if possible, from your original purchase. This will allow considerably more flexibility and opportunity for a variety of projects with both interior and exterior shots. If you were satisfied with the brand of the initial camera, you will probably want to remain with that company's newer models within your budget. Shop around for the best buy—a camera that gives you the features you want and that will help you enhance the quality of your video projects.

A second VCR with playback/record editing capabilities will now become essential if you are to produce projects such as classbooks and newscasts and to teach students more about the technology. A third VCR clearly provides even more flexibility.

An editor controller is another important component for even the simplest of editing. There are many types and brands; it is probably to your advantage to purchase components that are compatible to other pieces of equipment and made by the same company, although much of the equipment from different companies can be interfaced.

Editing control technology has changed dramatically in the past decade, going from "kerchunk"—manual editing on the fly—to highly sophisticated, multiple-source equipment totally controlled by computer. The main differences in editing systems are linear versus nonlinear, and analog versus digital. The trend is toward more high-tech, nonlinear, digital systems because of the seamless accuracy that these systems offer as well as the ability to add, delete, and modify video. Depending on your budget and your school's video goals, it would be good to work with people familiar with computers, perhaps colleagues who teach computer classes at your school, if you are considering computerized editing.

There are noncomputerized editing systems on the market that are much less expensive and that can perform with excellent results. These systems simply require more manual operation than the computer systems, but they can still deliver frame accuracy, an important standard by which most editors judge editing equipment.

Complementary to video editing devices (editor controllers) are digital video/audio mixers that include many special effects functions that can make simple source video look professionally produced. Another auxiliary component to the controller and mixer is the character generator that allows for many different titling and text functions to be presented as a part of the video, either as separate screens or keyed (overlayed electronically) over video.

Audio is an important part of video production. If you started with one or two microphones, you may want to add a few more: lavalieres for interviews, a shotgun microphone for shooting general audio in large areas from a distance, and a desk mike. In purchasing microphones, you get what you pay for. Good microphones are not inexpensive, but the difference in quality and service is usually worth the price.

You may want eventually to consider wireless microphones. They have improved considerably in recent years and allow flexibility that is valuable in and out of the classroom.

Additional TV monitors, an audio mixer, a music/sound effects library—the list is as long as the change in technology is rapid. They all make a contribution to a well-equipped operation.

In considering all of these additions and upgrades to your video and audio equipment inventory, it is important to remember that they can all be obtained in time. It is better for students and teachers to use basic equipment and learn to get maximum technical and artistic results from it than to start with all the bells and whistles. For an example of how one school district gradually added to its video equipment, see Figure 6.3.

FIGURE

6.3

Suggested Television Studio Equipment for Schools

The following list of equipment was compiled by Ed Seeley, media production specialist, of the Seminole County Public Schools, Sanford, Florida. This is the list of suggested equipment used by schools in the Seminole County school district as they gradually build their television production capabilities.

Stage 1 is the beginning stage, where video production is being done "off a cart" and stored "in a closet." *Note:* In addition to the recommended equipment listed, you may want to begin with remote broadcasting capability so you can broadcast programs throughout the school. To do this, your school facility must also have closed circuit television (CCTV) capability to receive a live video signal into each classroom. This will require additional hardware and wiring throughout your school.

Stage 1 Equipment List for Basic Level with Remote Broadcasting Capabilities

(1) VHS video camcorder (to photograph on air talent)

(1) Camera tripod (designed for use with camcorders to provide stable camera shots)

(1) 13" color video monitor (to monitor broadcast as it is being sent out live from your location)

(1) Projector cart (to store and transport equipment)

(1) Desk/handheld microphone (to connect to microphone cable)

(1) Tabletop microphone stand (to hold handheld microphone)

(1) 25' microphone cable (XLR) (to connect microphone to audio cable adapter)

(1) Audio Cable Adapter (to connect microphone cable into camcorder microphone input)

(1) RF modulator field unit (to send audio and video signals back to your head-end CCTV system)

(1) 25' video/audio cable (to connect camcorder to RF modulator field unit)

(1) 25' antenna cable (to connect RF modulator unit to an antenna wall outlet located near broadcasting area)

(1) Multiple outlet power strip (to plug in video production equipment)

(1) 25' heavy duty power extension cord (to supply power to power strip unit)
    Miscellaneous cables and connectors

At Stage 2 a room needs to be dedicated to video production and storage of the equipment on carts. The following equipment is added to the Stage 1 list:

(1) VHS video camcorder (a second camcorder in studio and for field news reports)

(1) Camera tripod (to support second camcorder)

(1) Production console (to support the various pieces of equipment)

(1) Character generator (to superimpose titles over video and to add text information)

(1) Digital video mixer (to use two cameras simultaneously with various special effects)

(1) Audio mixer (to mix several audio sources, such as mikes, VCRs, CD player, and so on, at once)

FIGURE

6.3

(continued)

(2) 13" color video monitors (for previewing titles, video mixing, on-air monitoring, and next stage editing)

(1) VHS playback unit (to playback field news footage during the newscast)

(1) Portable video lighting kit (for studio lighting as well as location lighting for on-air talent)

(4) Lapel Microphones (used for on-air talent)

(4) Microphone cables (connect microphones to the audio mixer)

(1) CD player (to play background music over newscast and other productions)

(1) Collection of copyright CDs from Music Library Company (allows you to use original music sound tracks legally cleared from copyright infringement laws)

Miscellaneous cables and connectors

Stage 3 involves dedicating a television studio to the production of video and live broadcasting. The following equipment is added to the Stage 1 and 2 equipment list:

(1) S-VHS editing system (to videotape field news footage and other productions)

(1) TelePrompTer (for on-air talent to read the news script from the TelePrompTer screen directly into the camera instead of from a written script on the desk.)

(1) TV news desk with 6" platform riser (for a professional-looking environment for your student news show)

(3) Scenic backdrops and croma key background (for different set design looks and croma key capability)

Miscellaneous cables and connectors

Note: During the planning phase of new construction or renovation, schools are designing studio-size environment into their facilities. This studio space consists of a separate studio and control room with a see-through window. It is recommended that a new studio facility be located in or near the school media center. A centrally located studio provides easy access for students and teachers plus security for equipment as well as control over what goes out over the airways for viewing. Only a few upgrades would be required such as premise wiring, studio intercom system, grid style lighting, and upgrades from camcorders to studio camera systems.

Choose one of the long-term projects described in this chapter and plan the steps required to implement it. Make a list of the people who would be involved in the project and the equipment that would be needed. Research the cost of the basic equipment that would be needed and the additional equipment you would buy as more money becomes available. Determine the steps needed to get the project up and running. Write a basic funding proposal using all the information you have gathered as if you were applying for a grant.

VIDEO PRACTICE ACTIVITY

Video Project
Using the research you did in the practice activity, create a script and storyboard for a presentation to your principal or school board requesting funds for your project. Videotape the presentation after you have completed the storyboard and collected the visuals and props needed. Evaluate your video after you have filmed it and use the in-camera editing techniques you have learned to improve the quality of the tape. If you are satisfied with the tape and are motivated to implement your project, show the video to your principal and ask for support in obtaining funds for the equipment you need.

USING VIDEO IN TEACHER REFLECTION AND EVALUATION

The use of videotaped lessons in the classroom for the purpose of teacher reflection and improvement of teaching strategies is an important aspect of video use in the schools. Many teachers and teacher education institutions have discovered the power of self-evaluation of lessons. Teachers working together in teams to support one another as they view themselves presenting lessons has shown to be a highly effective way to build teacher teams and improve instruction (Herrell, 1997).

Grade level or subject matter teams working together to provide video taping of lessons, small group viewing, and critiquing of video lessons supports the improvement of teaching strategies as well as the sharing of unique approaches to teaching, problem solving related to discipline and classroom management, and collaborative efforts to integrate curriculum.

Teachers who are dedicated to the improvement of teaching and curriculum planning will find the video camera a valuable resource. In addition, the way teachers approach teaching subjects in the classroom and sharing of these ideas differ. Demonstrating these ways on videotape can be valuable resources for inservice teachers, new teachers, substitute teachers, and teachers in training.

SUMMARY

The use of video in long-range and schoolwide projects has endless possibilities. Just making a video becomes an integrated curriculum project since it involves collaborative planning, writing a script, drawing a storyboard, rehearsing parts, and developing content to be videotaped. Videos make good culminating activities for thematic studies because each member of the class can be involved and all students end up with a copy of the product. The product is available for multiple viewings, and reflection and evaluation opportunities abound.

School-parent-community involvement projects involving video give many opportunities to strengthen public relations. Parents and community members are often not aware of the activities going on in the schools. Making a video demonstrating school activities and projects gives parents and community members a chance to actually see them and learn how they benefit the community as a whole. Showing these videos at community functions helps to encourage a broader community involvement.

Videos are effective methods to share teaching and learning strategies with parents and to provide teacher education and orientations to school and various programs within the school or school improvement projects. They also provide effective ways to share information and expertise with students, teachers, parents, and community members.

These projects and ones that are student centered, such as video classbooks, video time capsules, and school television stations, are made possible by training students in script writing, storyboarding, and video production skills. An elective class or after-school video production club is a valuable resource for the teachers and administrators and supports efforts in video projects across the school.

Beginning the use of video production in a school setting requires the purchase of basic equipment that can be expanded with the gradual addition of other camcorders, VCRs, monitors, and editing equipment over time. The effort to include video production in the curriculum provides many opportunities to teach, motivate students, and document learning.

REFERENCES

Egan, C. L. (1996). Video looping or continuous video playback, *Personal Communication*. Fresno: California State University Academic Innovation Center.

Herrell, A. (1997). Using video to improve teacher education. *Journal of Teacher Education 36* (2), 23–28.

Valmont, W. J. (1996). *Creating Videos for School Use.* Boston, MA: Allyn and Bacon.

SUGGESTED READINGS

Adams, D. (1988). A low cost production model for small format video production. *Tech Times, 33* (1), 17–22.

Anderson, G., and Balog, P. (1994, January/February). Equipment for in-school broadcasting studios. *Media and Methods*, 15–17.

Baraloto, R.A., and Silvious, S. (1991). 1 + 1 + 30 = Instructional Success. *School Library Media Activities Monthly, 7* (1), 36–38.

Ekhaml, L. (1995). Things the teacher of your media utilization course may not have told you. *School Library Media Activities Monthly, 11*(10), 31–36+.

Fortier, M. (1996). Creating a multimedia classbook. *Media and Methods, 33* (1), 20–22.

Greenwood, T. W. (1995, February). Let's pop some corn and watch your report card. *T.H.E. Journal.*

Hargis, M. (1990, May/June) The video yearbook. *Media and Methods*, 20–21.

Johnson, P. (1989). Rich encounters with television. *Media and Methods, 26* (2), 31–32+.

Jordahl, G. (1995, May/June). School-grown videos. Technology and Learning.

Lamme, L. (1988). *Learning to Love Literature.* Washington, DC: International Reading Association.

Millerson, G. (1992). *Video Production Handbook.* 2nd. ed. Oxford, MA: Focal Press.

Sulzby, E. (1991). Emergent stroybook reading stages. *The Readding Teacher 44* (3). 363–367.

Tovey, J. (1996). Must see TV: Making the most of schoolwide video systems. *Media and Methods, 33* (2), 12–14.

Video Resources

BASIC EQUIPMENT

The Camcorder

Every electronics manufacturer that produces camcorders in its equipment inventory designs them differently and includes just enough "bells and whistles" to be competitive in the dynamic video marketplace. Most of the basic components—the ones that really make the camera work—are pretty much the same, no matter what the name brand. For our purposes, information is confined to the *camcorder*, the camera and recorder in a single, self-contained unit.

Historically, before camcorders, there was the camera as a separate unit umbilicated by a cable (that never seemed to be long enough) to a recorder, usually hung over the shoulder and it was heavy and cumbersome.

With the development of "small format video" camcorders, it seemed that "easy" video production became accessible to everyone, individuals, schools, small businesses and professions, artists, churches, and others who wanted to use the medium. It was small, it was portable, and it was relatively inexpensive.

The basic components of typical camcorder models, whether Super-VHS (S-VHS), VHS, 8mm, Hi8, or VH-C include these:

- Battery pack
- Built-in stereo microphone
- Built-in speaker
- Viewfinder
- Power switch
- Zoom lens
- Audio selector switch
- Manual iris open/close button
- Auto white balance
- AC adapter
- Accessory shoe
- Lens hood/cap
- Cassette compartment
- S-VHS/VHS system selector switch
- Manual or auto focus
- Iris shutter speed adjustment

- Date/time setting button
- On-screen display button
- Audio dubbing button
- Memory button
- Reset button
- Cable/connector pack
- Flying erase-head

- Manual fade from/ to black
- Rewind/review, play, pause, fast forward, still advance, and stop buttons
- Carrying case

In addition, most camcorder models have several jack positions for functions such as auxiliary microphone, editing, video output, audio output, radio frequency (RF) and direct current (DC) output (used when you want to hook the camera directly to the monitor to view what you have recorded), remote control, character generator, and DC input. All camcorders have a receptacle beneath the camera body for attaching tripod screws.

Battery Power Versus AC Adapter

Another feature of portability in the camcorder is battery operation. A battery can be attached to or inserted into the camera, depending on the camera model. At least one battery is generally part of the camcorder package, but it is a good idea to purchase a few additional ones. The life of a camcorder battery is usually mentioned in the camcorder owner's manual; the average life today is about two hours before it needs recharging, but different uses of the camcorder can make that time significantly lower. An indicator in the camera's viewfinder screen indicates when the battery is low or empty. Most camcorder batteries need to be fully discharged before recharging to prolong the capacity of the battery.

When it is time to recharge, batteries can be attached to the AC adapter unit that comes with the camcorder package and plugged into any AC electrical outlet. The adapter unit indicates when the battery is charging and when it has been fully charged. This unit not only serves as a recharger for the battery but also as a connector for AC power. Some batteries require full discharge before recharging. Check your operations manual for instructions for your battery.

Whenever possible during shooting, remove the battery from the camera and use the AC adapter. A cable that leads from the camera into the adapter is provided in each camcorder package. The adapter can be plugged into an electrical outlet, and power is as unlimited as the electrical current running through the room. Use of the adapter, as you might have noted, limits the movement of the camera somewhat since it is tied to an electrical cord. Extension cords add flexibility, but you still must tote the AC adapter unit when you move. This is a trade-off: unlimited power versus restrictive tethering. At the end of a shoot when using battery power, always remove the battery from the camera, discharge and recharge it if necessary, and store it in a cool, dry place until its next use.

The Video Cassette Recorder

A VCR (video cassette recorder) machine is an essential companion to the camcorder. Although material technically can be recorded and played back directly from the camcorder to a TV monitor with correct cables and connectors, this is awkward. Viewing the tape with a VCR is much more convenient.

There are standard features on virtually all VCRs that allow recording playback of videotape. Nearly all VCRs have a built-in time base connector (TBC) that is a device that stabilizes the video signal and keeps it from fluttering and rolling. Editing on a VCR cannot be accomplished without a TBC.

There are choices of video and audio inputs, front or rear. While the functions are standard, the sophistication of the inputs varies from brand to brand and model to model. Ask a VCR salesperson to explain what the different VCRs are capable of providing and match the information with your needs. Get the best machine that you can afford.

Audio Equipment

Every camcorder has a built-in microphone that is adequate for most shooting situations. The camera mike, however, is limited in distance range so that placement of the camera in relation to any person that you want to hear clearly becomes a major consideration. Another major drawback in using the built-in mike is that it picks up all noise within its range, including background noise. In the classroom this can be a big consideration.

To cut down on background noise and ensure that the video is clear, an auxiliary microphone is a wise addition to your equipment inventory. Every camcorder is equipped to accept at least one microphone input. When you use an auxiliary mike, this bypasses the built-in mike circuitry and this allows for more distinctive audio when that is important to your production. Generally, auxiliary microphones are more sensitive in range so that they can pick up audio sources from greater distances than the built-in camera mike. This could be important when the teacher's instructions as well as responses need to be heard from the microphone's primary subject.

If your budget can afford it, purchase *two* auxiliary mikes: a lavaliere-type "personal" microphone that can be clipped onto a person's clothing or hung around the neck, and a hand-held microphone that can also be used as a desk mike. Be certain that whatever microphone you buy has the proper connectors—jack plug-in—for your model camera. The lavaliere microphone allows for one-on-one interaction (for example, interviews with a student), and the hand-held/desk mike provides an audio source for group interaction.

When purchasing auxiliary microphones, you may want to ask about extra mike cord lengths that would give you greater flexibility in shooting situations. You may also want to check out wireless microphones; their circuitry and reliability have improved greatly in recent years, and they could provide maximum range flexibility.

Lighting Equipment

Most classrooms were not built with television production in mind. Therefore, the lighting, while adequate for normal class activities, is not necessarily adequate for quality video shoots. For most shooting situations, this does not present a problem: you are not, after all, attempting to achieve broadcast-quality video, but you do want to ensure that your video will not be too dark to view and that your students do not reproduce on videotape in silhouette!

Most camcorders nowadays are designed with low-light conditions in mind. You can achieve some remarkable video resolution with what appears to the human eye to be very little light.

If your classroom shooting area appears to be dimly lit, you may want to look into buying some professional lighting fixtures on extension stands from a photo store or from a video lighting manufacturer. Many retail outlets that sell consumer-grade video equipment also stock some lighting equipment. When you are looking for lighting equipment, keep in mind the safety features: most professional lighting fixtures can reach very high and, thereby, dangerous, temperature levels. There are fixtures and lamps on the market that provide strong light without hot temperatures. These obviously would be preferred, although they probably could be more expensive than other lighting instruments. Two fixtures—lamps and stands—should be an adequate lighting inventory for most shooting situations.

COMPOSITION

If you are shooting people or objects for TV, there are certain composition elements that are important to remember so that when your videotape is played back on any size screen, your images are very close to the way you had originally framed them in the camera.

Rule of Thirds (explain meaning)

Using the TV aspect ratio and dividing the rectangular box equally into thirds both horizontally and vertically, the intersecting points of the lines represent important focal areas in the frame. This is known as the *rule of thirds.* This can sometimes be helpful in composing shots with people and objects to achieve the most pleasing balance of elements in the frame.

Subservience Versus Dominance and the Diagonal in All of Us

In framing for effect, raise the camera as high as you can and shoot down on a subject to show subservience or inferiority. To show the opposite, dominance, shoot from a very low angle upward toward the subject.

To achieve a strong dynamic effect in a shot, place your subjects or objects along an imaginary diagonal line from any corner of the frame.

For peace and tranquillity, position subjects in the shot in a horizontal orientation. For a more uplifting effect, line up the subjects vertically.

Positioning people in a triangular pattern with the bottom row seated and graduated rows of people above is usually a pleasing composition.

Practice with different symmetrical and asymmetrical placements of people and objects to determine what works best for your projects. The bottom line is that if a shot is pleasing to your eye, it usually is a good sign that elements of composition are working well.

Aspect Ratio

Television pictures, or the way we see them, are contained in a frame that is three units high by four units wide (3:4). This is a very broad definition of *aspect ratio*. This ratio applies from the camcorder viewfinder to the largest standard TV set screen manufactured.

When composing TV images, you must think about keeping all of the essential information—subjects, objects, graphics, and so on—within the relatively narrow confines of those horizontally oriented, 3:4 dimensions. Many camcorder viewfinders are calibrated to show the operator guidelines within which to compose a scene. All essential information should be kept within these guidelines so that when the videotape is played back on any standard TV monitor—no matter what its dimensions may be—the same visual information that was seen through the camera's small viewfinder is reproduced in basically the same position on the larger TV screen.

BASIC PREPRODUCTION, PRODUCTION, AND POSTPRODUCTION TECHNIQUES

Preproduction

Not enough can be said about the importance of preproduction, the planning that is essential to any successful video project. Perhaps the best advice to follow when planning a classroom video project is to keep it simple. There are many things to consider when planning a video production. A preproduction checklist is a handy way to insure that you remember everything.

- *The physical logistics.* Planning where the shooting will take place is an important part of preproduction. If you need to move the camera around, are the aisles cleared? Is there enough light, or will additional lights have to be provided?
- *Talent.* This refers to anyone who will appear on camera, your students, guest speakers, and/or entertainers or artists. They need to be rehearsed if necessary, certainly in place as a part of the preproduction run-through.
- *Director.* This is the person who will be giving the production crew and talent their directions. This may be the teacher, a parent, or one of the students.
- *Script.* This is the "spine" of the television production. It provides the dialogue and guidelines for camera movements, shots, and scene and time elements of the production.
- *A prop list.* A list of props including such items as books, costumes, and furniture—from the smallest to the largest items—that must be gathered and made available as a part of preproduction.
- *Still pictures and graphics.* These can be used for the title of the production or to show a transition to another time frame (signs saying, for example, "Later That Day" or "Many Years Later").
- *Storyboards.* Small panels of drawn action with dialogue or other written explanation tell the continuous story on paper before it is committed to video or film. Story boards serve as the initial visualization of the script.

Very few directors attempt to begin any project without a storyboard. From the storyboards, the director composes the final shots through the camera lens. The notes on the storyboard identify the distance and movement of the camera, as well as the accompanying dialogue.

Storyboard art does not have to be professional; stick figures have done the job many times. It is important, however, to be accurate with the placement of the figures and objects in each storyboard panel. Otherwise, you will not have models from which to compose your camera shots. In the classroom sometimes you will want to do a series of informal interviews with students for which a detailed storyboard for each interview may not be necessary or even possible. Just a mental note to do a series of head-and-shoulder shots with appropriate close-ups on the students' work may be all that is needed.

Once you have taken care of all the preproduction details, make a *final inventory of your equipment*—camcorder, tripod, audio (using an auxiliary mike today?) cables, maybe a lighting instrument over in that corner. Don't forget to put a fresh video-tape into the camera carrier. These are all a part of the preproduction countdown.

You still have a few minutes to do a *shakedown*: ask Susie to read a few lines from her book while you record some video-tape. Yes, the lens cap is off. "Thank you, Susie." Stop the tape, rewind it, and then view it on *playback* through the camera's viewfinder and listen to the audio from the tiny earplug that you have placed into the ear receptacle on the camera. Yes! Crisp video and clear audio! Rewind the tape again and run off about 15 seconds of tape with the lens cap back on. Stop tape. You are ready. Countdown: 10–9–8–7–6–5–4–3–2–1....(Don't forget to take the lens cap off!)

It's production time! And it all begins to gel.

Production

To actually shoot the video, you will refer to your script and storyboard. The storyboard includes planned video shots and camera movements to create a smooth sequence. Shot size and camera movements are an important part of the plan. The production phase involves following the script and storyboard and getting everything on videotape. Depending on the editing equipment you have available, you will either follow the sequence of shots very carefully, editing in-camera or shoot the scenes as convenient and use your editing equipment to assemble the tape in correct sequence. (See editing explanations later in the chapter.)

Postproduction

Editing

Video editing can be examined from two perspectives; technical and aesthetic. The two go hand-in-hand.

Technical   Most camcorders on the market today have editing and special transitional effects functions as standard features. When shopping around for a camcorder, you should try to purchase one with as many of the following functions as possible:

- *Basic video/audio dubbing functions.* They allow the camcorder to be plugged in to a VCR and/or audio mixer to make duplicate copies of video or for adding voice-over narration or music.
- *Flying erase heads.* With this function, you can shoot a new segment immediately following a previous one without a glitch—technical "snow"—in your picture. The *pause button* on the camera, in effect, becomes an editor controller: you press pause when you end a shot and again when you start shooting the new segment.
- *Fade-to/from black.* This is for transition between shots and segments. *Fade from black* indicates a beginning; *fade to black* indicates an ending.
- *Still function.* Use this to "freeze" a particular shot for whatever time desired and without interruption for audio recording.
- *Strobe effect.* This is used to take out frames of motion to present a type of animation effect. Some cameras have different strobe speeds available.
- *Pattern or mosaic effect.* It transforms images into colored shapes composed of electronic tiles whose size can be manipulated from sharp to soft edged.

Aesthetic   The aesthetics of editing is the artistic interpretation of video story telling suggested by certain guidelines of pictorial composition, sequencing, and pacing, some of which have been mentioned earlier. The same aesthetics considerations apply whether you are editing in-camera or with sophisticated electronic postproduction equipment.

Traditionally, you will want your video story to have a beginning, a middle, and an end. You must also keep the eventual viewer of your video piece in mind. Assume that that person or audience knows little or nothing about the subject your video is about. You must be able to lead the viewer from a logical point A to points B, C, and so on, and sometimes you will do it with pictures—video—only. You must also show the viewer all of the elements you think are important to see in a sequence that is easy to follow and understand. You cannot use any subject or procedure that is familiar to you and assume that it is also familiar to the viewer. For example, you see your classroom every day and know each detail of its order: Where every student sits; where the books are stored; what shelves the art supplies are in, and so on. You know its relationships. In a video that will be seen by an audience of parents who have never visited your classroom, you must be prepared to express this familiarity through your video, and the way you shoot it to tell "its story" could mean the difference between comprehension and confusion. This is a basic lesson in video aesthetics and editing.

Always show the viewers where you are by using an *establishing shot.* This may mean first shooting the outside of the school building, showing its name. Then bring the viewers inside the building and show the principal standing outside the office motioning you to enter. The nest scene shows the principal sitting at his desk and the dialogue begins. Figure A.1 shows the storyboard for this sequence.

F I G U R E   *Examples of Wide Establishing Shot Moving to Closer Shot to Set the Stage*
A.1

Shoot a wide shot of the classroom; you want your picture to be steady (jiggling pictures can "turn off" viewers) and to last as long as you think it would take for a viewer to absorb all the necessary information but not so long as to risk boring the viewer. That's another aesthetic decision.

The next segment you shoot might focus on a specific student or object in the classroom that was included in your wide shot. You are telling your viewer to "follow me; I'm showing you the important things" in this sequence. Then you may begin a new sequence of shots that represent the next phase of your narrative or storyline.

From time to time, you may want to reinforce some of your shots with *cut-ins, cut-outs,* and/or *cutaways.* Let's say that you recorded a wide shot that included a student with a book on her desk. Your next segment was a medium shot of the area where the student is seated, showing the book. If the book is an important element in the sequence, the next shot could be a cut-in—an extreme closeup of the book—showing its cover, title, and so on, shot in the same contextual and physical relationship as seen in the preceding medium shot. The next shot, a cut-out, will be basically the same medium shot of the student that preceded the cut-in, picking up on whatever activity or movement has occurred in real time. This is a way to lead the viewer into and out of an element of a shot that you consider important.

Cutaway shots can be anything that helps to further explain elements in your sequence or to show another event or activity that is happening simultaneously. In their most conventional form, cutaway shots may be difficult to achieve while shooting and editing in-camera because you run the risk of losing the continuity of important audio each time you pause the camera to reset for the next shot. For example, the video storyline has the teacher explaining the capital cities of each state. Ideally, as she is naming each capital, you would want to show a picture—a cutaway shot—of the city or its capitol building. Even if you had still pictures of the capital cities or capitol buildings all lined up near your camera, you would have to pause your camera, set up on one of the pictures, shoot it for a few seconds, then reset on the teacher, and follow this sequence for as long as you wanted shots of the capitals/capitols. However, to maintain continuity of the teacher's lecture—the audio part of the sequence—she would have to pause also to allow for the next camera shot to be set up before proceeding. This could be awkward and could be distracting enough to cause students in the class to lose interest.

Cutaways are best used in postproduction editing, which we will discuss in a moment. A variation of the cutaway, using the same setup as described here, can be achieved simply by panning over to each picture as it is being described by the teacher and panning back to the teacher. You must be careful about staying in focus while panning back and forth between two subject areas, even if the distances between seem small.

Reaction shots are a form of cutaways. They often are used to show a person or persons (an audience) listening to a speaker and reacting to the speech with some facial expression, either neutral, or smiling, laughing, frowning, and so on. The same procedure that applies to cutaways in in-camera editing shooting would work here, except that the camera will probably have to be panned with an even larger arc than when shooting prearranged still pictures. In any situation where pans or tilts are used, do them slowly; otherwise, the audience may be suddenly jolted from an otherwise smooth sequence with a swish pan or tilt.

One important technique to remember about using audience shots as cutaways is to allow for viewer perspective. Let's say you are shooting a speaker who is predominately on the left side of your camcorder's viewfinder. You have composed the shot well, giving the speaker a little headroom and some nose room, or look space. When you shoot your audience, make sure that it is being framed to appear to be looking from screen right, at the speaker, even though that person is not shown in the frame. In other words, shoot the audience at roughly the opposite angle and composition from the one showing the speaker. This is particularly critical when editing in postproduction. There have been many instances when the audience shots were recorded at different times than when a specific speaker was shot addressing it. Unless the camera operator remembered her camera position in relationship to the speaker, sometimes the audience was shot looking in the same direction as the person speaking, thereby making the audience shots useless as reactions, or cutaways.

Continuity and direction of action are very important to the natural flow of your video piece. If you shoot a wide shot of someone beginning to sit down in a chair, the next shot of that person should show him finishing the action by being shown sitting down into the chair, not already seated. If you show a person moving off screen toward the *right,* the next shot of the same person should show her entering from screen *left.* Don't show someone walking casually in one shot only to have the same person running in the next one.

For transitions, that is, getting from one sequence or shot to a different sequence or shot, you may use the camera special effects features that are included in nearly every camcorder nowadays.

The fade to black/from black feature should be used sparingly. In video protocol, black signifies a definite end—to a shot, a sequence, or a whole video story. It is effective but can be overused or abused and can be confusing to a viewer.

An example of a correct time to use black is when the teacher is preparing portfolios in individual students. Each segment should end on black, signifying that a specific portfolio has been completed. A fade up from black indicates new material and a new student until the next fade to black is evident, and so forth.

Also, when all the elements of a specific assignment or exercise have been discussed, or played out, or simply recorded for archival and storage purposes, a fade to black means that package is complete.

Use black between interview segments, when you want to add a "commercial" or public service announcement, and return to the interview. Often your last shot, perhaps a medium close-up of the interviewer before fading to black, is also your opening shot when fading up from black.

If a shooting situation—say a performance—calls for it, you could choose the pattern or mosaic special effects between scenes, although this device should be used even more sparingly than the fade to/from black.

The so-called strobe effect is actually a high-speed shutter feature on some camcorders. You can set the camera to record certain intervals of images and, when played back, it appears that the person or subject is in slowed-down, somewhat jerky, motion. This can be a useful technique when demonstrating such activities as a golf club swing or a tennis serve.

One of the few times that a swish pan is effective is for transition from one point to another, but for the effect to work properly, you need to practice it a few times before committing it to videotape; timing and distance from two points are the crucial elements.

Practice also makes the rack focus transition technique more effective. It usually involves zooming into and defocusing on a subject to a point where the image is indistinguishable, and then changing the subject while still defocused and slowly zooming out and refocusing to basically the same composition and framing as the previous shot.

Other transition devices, such as title cards, clock faces with hands moved, or rapid swish-pans, can further explain your story to a viewer. Use your imagination on visual graphics; they can be fun to produce, and they can enhance the overall look of your production.

Keep in mind that all of these transition devices and techniques are most effective if they will help the viewer to distinguish between various segments of a video sequence. However, the more "devices" that are used during in-camera shooting and editing, the more carefully planned your camerawork and all other production aspects need to be.

Using the script in Figure A.2, followed by the instructions, you can practice your in-camera editing techniques. Two options, assemble editing and insert editing, can be used to produce this piece, one more complex than the other, but both are designed to give you some experience in editing in-camera.

Video editing, by its most simplistic definition, is the process by which you put selected segments of audio and video material in the order in which you want them seen. Many experienced producers of video believe that postproduction, of which editing is an integral part, is where video programs are fine-tuned with the polish and "pizzazz" that the final product reflects. These production veterans would probably also be the first to caution that editing cannot correct all mistakes that may have been made during production or pull segments out of the air like a rabbit out of a magician's hat. However, editing can take material that has been well produced and, through technical and aesthetic manipulation, can usually make the video the best it can be.

*School
Orientation
Video Script*

VIDEO	AUDIO
WS front of school showing children entering (Aprx :07)	Welcome to Friendly School.
Outside MS of office (Aprx :07) (:15) *	We'd like to tell you more about our school. Here's our principal.
MS principal standing by desk: (Aprx :10) (*Note:* You will shoot both audio and video in real time; it is called SOT (sound on tape)	Hello. I'm Edward Educator, principal of Friendly School. I'd like to welcome you to our school and let you know that I'm available to talk to you about any concerns.
Zoom in to MCU of principal (Aprx :08) (:15)**	
(WS of classroom) (Aprx: :15)	You may notice that the classroom is laid out differently than when you were in school.
	The desks are in clusters so that the children can work together on projects. I'd like for you to see some classroom scenes so that you will be familiar with the kind of work your child will be doing this year.
Children enter classroom picking up journals and sitting down to write (Aprx :16)	We start the day with journal writing. Children are responsible for getting their journals and writing daily about something in which they are interested. This journal writing is often used as the start of a book, poem, or play.
Children put journals away; gather on carpet for opening exercises (Aprx :08)	After the children write in their journals, they meet to officially begin their day.
Pledge to the flag; calendar; reading (Aprx :08)	They recite the pledge to the flag . . . check the calendar. . .read aloud.
Children move to their desks, get out folders and begin to read and write, alone and in groups. (Aprx: 17)	After opening exercises, the children are involved in a period of active reading and writing we call Reading/Writing Workshop. This looks very different than the old reading groups you probably experienced when you were in school.
Parent and teacher talking, teacher showing parent around the class. (Aprx :14)	If you have any questions about why things are being done or if you would like to visit the classroom, please feel free to call and make an appointment.
Fade to black:	Thank you.

*Although the script calls for :07 of this shot, shoot for :15.
**Let the tape roll for an additional :08.

Most long-time users of video recommend that editing equipment be a part of the overall production inventory. There is more and more support for this as prices for some fairly sophisticated postproduction equipment continue to come down.

This segment focuses on both in-camera editing in situations when you are actually making a determined selection of material as you are shooting and editing as a postproduction procedure.

In-camera editing   If editing equipment cannot be an initial item in your school's video equipment budget, you must rely on good planning and the in-camera, or editing-while-you-shoot method.

Editing in-camera has an obvious benefit of producing a first-generation videotape: Everything is being shot and recorded for the first time and could be played back on the same videotape. We discuss tape generations later.

Some of the disadvantages of editing in-camera include the fact that you must shoot everything in a certain sequence, usually ordered by a script; you do not have the advantage of shooting multiple takes of each shot and later choosing only the best of the lot. You are limited to shooting once without stopping or stopping and rewinding and starting all over again; the timing and length of each shot are important. And you are likely not going to have audio continuity in the background. Each time you record video, whatever sound is heard will be recorded as well and will probably sound choppy and interrupted when the finished tape is played back.

Yet another disadvantage is that you must work quickly and be prepared to shoot one person or subject, pause your camera, reset and focus and shoot the next segment, all before the automatic pause mechanism in your camcorder shuts down and, in effect, turns off your camera. When this occurs, the next time you start the camera, the videotape will rewind itself back to a spot seconds before the end of your previous shot and you likely will have lost the tail end of it. It is difficult, if not impossible, to achieve any kind of accurate frame editing using the in-camera method.

The preproduction planning mentioned in Chapter 1 is of paramount importance to in-camera editing; a basic script and a storyboard are two indispensable elements. Logistical planning in the classroom is at least as important as well; placement of students, props, and graphics must be well planned, if not choreographed, and, continuity—the natural flow of your story line with all of its visual elements—becomes key.

Editing Option 1
Step 1

Prerecord the *audio* on a portable cassette recorder (including the SOT segment that you will also record on videotape). Play the audio tape back and time each segment with a stopwatch. The actual time it takes to speak the narration plus 2 seconds on either end of the segments is the actual time of your video segments when you shoot them.

> **Example:** "Welcome to Friendly School" times out at about 2.5 seconds. By adding 2 seconds on either end of that piece of narration (4 seconds total), your video segment will last about 6.5 seconds, rounded off to 7 seconds. You want to allow more time for the video than the actual audio time for purposes of in-camera editing and pacing.

Step 2

Storyboard the script, scene by scene. *(This is the information under the left, or video column of the script).* (See Figure A.2). The storyboard does not have to be elaborately drawn; stick figures will do. The purpose is to give you a visual idea on paper of what you want the video composition to look like. It also allows you to avoid any "bad" composition or continuity such as a jump cut.

Step 3

Shoot the first scene on a tripod outside the school. (*Pause* the camera and move quickly inside, camera still on the tripod, secured, to shoot Scene 2.) (Alternate shot: Instead of pausing the camera, let the videotape continue to roll and walk into the building keeping the camera as steady as you can.)

Step 4

(Hit *Pause* to activate *Record* for the scene outside the principal's office). (*Note:* Although the script calls for :07 of the office shot, shoot that scene for about 15 seconds to allow for smoother editing later.) *Stop the camera* after shooting this scene.

Step 5

As the producer/director, you should have given the principal a copy of the script well in advance of the shooting day with your direction as to how you plan to shoot the sequence, how he should pause in his narration occasionally, and how he should look the camera in its "eye" because it represents the parents that he will be talking to.

Step 6

Set up your camera on a tripod. Ideally, the principal will have memorized the entire script, but if he is not a "quick study," you may have had to prepare cue cards for him. (Actually, he is *on camera* only for the short statement beginning with "Hello. I'm Edward. . ." and ending with ". . . when you were in school.")

Before the shoot, ask him to read the script distinctly at a moderate speaking rate, with natural pauses between paragraphs. *Time* him with a stopwatch as he reads and note the time it takes to read the on-camera part. Let him rehearse a few times if necessary because once you start the camera rolling, *you must record his on-camera narrative in one take*—nonstop.

Step 7

Play back the videotape of the first two scenes in your camcorder viewfinder. As the second scene plays, count to yourself (one thousand one, one-thousand two, etc.) for about 8 seconds, and then *pause* the tape. When the camera is ready to roll, hit the *pause* button and cue the principal at the same time. (See the hand signal cues in Figure 6.7 in Chapter 6.)

The script calls for a zoom in to an MCU of the principal. This is primarily to avoid a monotonous shot for too long, but it is an optional shot. (*Note:* Let the tape roll for another 7 seconds after the principal concludes.) *Stop the tape.*

Step 8

Record the remainder of the principal's narrative on cassette tape only. After the principal has given a flawless narrative, play it back to make sure the segment meets your needs and standards before you dismantle your equipment; you might not have another recording opportunity for a while. Be very careful of the videotape; you now have your first three scenes on it.

Step 9

With the help of the students in the class, the remainder of the shots need to be prearranged, or "staged," for the camera, to minimize camera movements and set-ups.

Step 10

Based on the timings on the script, shoot the remainder of the scenes in the classroom, pausing between each, and then pushing the *Pause* button again to reactivate the *Record* function until all the scenes have been recorded.

If there is a mistake made, you must locate an appropriate spot on the recorded tape and reshoot the scene as near to the original timing as possible and hope that the new material will cover the old without leaving a "false edit" blip, or a tape glitch.

Make a dub (copy) of the segment videotape as soon as possible after recording; set aside the original and use the dub in Step 11.

Step 11

Familiarize yourself with the operation of the *audio dub* function of your camera. It is explained in your camera's operation manual. Practice this function on the videotape dub you have made of the segments. This will allow you to check the audio dub function's accuracy as well as the timing and pacing of the audio and video segments together for the first time.

Cue up the audio tape as precisely as you can on the cassette machine. Using the cable and jack from the audio cassette machine, plug the jack into the *Audio Accessory* or *external* socket on the camcorder. Push the *audio dub* button on the camcorder and the *record* button, and then play back the cassette tape.

If everything has worked properly with the audio dub function, the previously recorded audio on the videotape should have been erased and replaced with the new audio fed from the cassette machine into the camcorder. If it has performed to your satisfaction, you are now ready to dub the audio onto the previously recorded original *master* videotape.

If Editing Option 1 seems complex, it is. But if similar procedures are performed a few times, the steps become much easier. This editing option demonstrates all of the elements that need to be carefully considered and planned for and shows the production demands that are an essential part of in-camera editing. (Documenting the difficulty of this procedure might also help in reinforcing your request for editing equipment.)

Editing Option 2   The basic production techniques in this option include shooting and editing in-camera segments of video that are not necessarily standard throughout the school but that could feature individual classroom activities. This option could include an SOT (sound on tape) segment of the principal, probably at the very beginning or maybe at the end; it could also allow a segment on the teacher, and it could feature more of the individual students in your class showing parents and other visitors the various activities that are special to your group; it could provide a preview of the kinds of lessons that are planned for the school session.

The main difference between producing a video in Editing Option 1 and in Option 2 is that in Option 2 the video segments can be more varied, shorter or longer, and instead of voice-over narration, the videotape can play while the scenes are explained with live narrative rather than with prerecorded audio dubbed onto the videotape.

The same careful planning must be observed in producing the Editing Option 2 video. As you can see, it allows more leeway in the kinds of video segments and in the audio presentation. You might have the class do both editing options and evaluate the end purposes and results of each.

Postproduction editing   Postproduction editing differs from in-camera editing in several important ways. The most obvious difference between the two editing methods is in the use of the equipment. In in-camera editing, a single camcorder, one VCR playback machine, and a monitor were used as separate units, each doing jobs specified for each piece of equipment.

In postproduction editing, however, the same two pieces of equipment can be put to use as a basic editing unit, if the camera doubles as a playback unit, and the VCR doubles as playback and record machines with interconnecting cables that are standard accessories in both camera and VCR purchases. The same procedures between a camcorder and a VCR machine will remain basically the same when we discuss editing between two VCR machines.

Here's how it works. The camera performs its traditional task, shooting all of the footage of the different scenes but with major differences from the restrictive in-camera shooting/editing. This time, you may shoot scenes as many times as you feel necessary, from as many different angles as you think might make the finished piece more interesting, and all of this may be done out of the scripted sequence of your storyline for the convenience of schedules, locations, and even weather. The camera shoots video that will become known as the *source tape,* segments from which will eventually be recorded onto the *master tape* as you tell your story, tape bit by tape bit, through editing.

To keep track of where the source material is located on the original videotape—the different scenes you have shot—it is a good, if not imperative, idea to *log* the videotape. Logging the videotaped footage involves writing down the VCR or camcorder counter time under *Time In* on the form when the sequence begins. The sequence ending time is written under *Time Out* when the scene is complete. Under *Description,* a brief description of the scene is written along with comments about the quality of the video and audio so the best video sequence can be chosen for the final video. See Figure A.3 for a sample of a Log Sheet. Rewind your source videotape in the VCR or, if one is available, a tape rewind machine. Use the VCR counter (if it is digital) or a stop watch and write down each segment as you view it for its position on the tape (from the head, or beginning of the videotape), time (length of the segment), and content (what is in the scene).

Blacking the Master Videotape

Video signals are always "flying wild" through the air. Very sophisticated equipment is used to "harness" video signals from the instant they are generated from a source to the time they appear on your TV screen at home. One of the most common ways to stabilize video signals on a more "domestic" level is by putting a black signal—one without any distinguishing video image—sometimes called *black burst* onto the videotape that will become the edited master tape. At video and television production facilities, this is done electronically through a constant signal generated electronically by a machine. Our method is a

F I G U R E

A.3

*Video
Project Log
Sheet*

Segment: _____

Tape # _____   Page # _____

Time In	Time Out	Description

lot more basic, but it helps ensure that the signal from the source tape will have the best chance of being transferred onto the master tape without interruption or interference or glitches.

First, put the master tape to be in the VCR and fast forward it. The tape usually automatically rewinds when it reaches its maximum length. This allows a new tape to "flex," or loosen, on its reels inside the cassette and helps prevent any stretching of the tape during the editing, when the master tape will be starting and stopping frequently.

Second, place the videotape into the camcorder and *cap the camera lens* tightly. Place a dummy micro jack into the external microphone socket on the camcorder or use any unconnected cable that has a microjack plug on the end of it. This procedure disengages, or cancels, the internal camera microphone system so that no unwanted sound is recorded onto the videotape during the blacking process.

Third, press *record* on the camera and let the videotape play for a time period a few minutes beyond the proposed length of your finished video program. For example, if you planned for a 6-minute finished video program, allow the tape to be blacked for 8 or 9 minutes, or even longer. This ensures plenty of black for your anticipated program length and gives you a little margin in case you change your mind and add several more video segments to the video piece. You may, of course, black the entire tape if you wish. Do not allow the camera to stop during the blacking process. If, for some reason, the camera does stop, rewind the tape or, preferably, get fresh videotape and repeat the blacking procedure until you have an uninterrupted blacked tape of the length desired. Stop the camcorder and eject the blacked videotape.

Next place the videotape in the VCR and rewind it to the "head of tape," the very beginning of the tape. Put the source tape, with all of the original footage on it, in your camcorder.

When you are ready to record on your blacked *master tape,* you simply interconnect the proper cables from the camera to the VCR according to your operator's manuals. Operator's manuals that now come with equipment are much easier to read and follow than they once were. They usually have pictures of each auxiliary piece, including the cables, that show how the interconnections are made. Generally, the cable jacks and sockets are readily identifiable with well-marked *in* and *out* labels for both video and audio.

You are now ready to begin editing. From your video Log Sheet, you see that Take 3 of the first segment that you want to put on the master is the best (because you made a notation to that effect when you were logging the original footage). Find the beginning of Take 3 and pause your camcorder. Acting quickly, forward the blacked master tape in the VCR about 10–15 seconds and *pause* it.

Press *record* on the VCR and then press *play* on the camcorder and let the two tapes roll until the scene from the source tape has played the desired length. It is all right to let the original, source tape play several seconds beyond the actual end of the scene onto the master tape. You can always go back to the correct spot on the master to begin the next edit.

When the edit has been made to your satisfaction, *stop* both camcorder and VCR. Look for the next scene on your camcorder based on your log sheet and continue the steps above until you have assembled all the desired video scenes, one after the other, that have now become your "seamless" edited video piece.

VCR-To-VCR Editing   In the previous discussion, it was mentioned that the camcorder was used in a configuration similar to that of a playback VCR. The major difference here, then, is that you may use two VCRs, one as a playback of your source tape, the other as a record machine. Of course, you will be able to use the knobs, dials, and buttons featured on the VCR machines, generally with increased speed and accuracy in your editing. Whereas the camcorder that you used as a VCR was only as fast as its internal playback mechanism, nearly all VCR machines have search knobs or dials that help in quickly finding locations on videotape.

The camcorder's viewfinder was used as a TV monitor when you were searching your source tape. For VCR-to-VCR editing, you will need two separate television monitors so you can see the output from each of the VCRs at the same time, and you will need an additional cable when you use the VCR-to-VCR option. However, there is little change in preparation and editing procedures per se between camcorder-VCR and VCR-to-VCR: Logging the original tape, blacking the master tape, fast forwarding, rewinding, and performing the actual edits will remain pretty much the same as you experienced if you used the camcorder as a playback VCR.

Now is probably the best time to explain the two types of video editing as we introduce higher levels of postproduction hardware in the discussion.

Assemble Editing

Assemble editing is fundamentally the procedure we have been discussing up to now: You literally build your video piece segment by segment, in the chronological order of your storyline.

You cannot change your mind and go back to replace an early segment that has already been laid onto the master tape without a "glitch," or video snow, on the tape.

Insert Editing

In the *insert edit* mode you have a great deal more flexibility and aesthetic control over how you edit your video. When you blacked the master tape prior to recording on it, it was, in effect, laying down a "control track," which allows you to place and re-place pieces of video electronically until you are satisfied with the final results.

For example, if you laid down 5 minutes of edited segments and you suddenly remembered a scene that you should have used about a minute into the videotape, you could go back and replace the original scene with the new material provided there was enough of the new video to occupy the same space as the first video you edited there. You would not have to worry about reediting the remaining 4 minutes that followed the newly inserted segment. On some older editing machines, it is crucial when employing insert editing that any new material be just slightly longer in time than the segment you are going to replace. Otherwise, you will get "flash frames" of old material on either end, or both, of the original material; you must be able to cover all of the old video, plus a little overlap, to make the edit appear seamless and glitchless. Insert editing allows you to add cutaway, reversal, and reaction shots and other video material such as graphics to a good program tape to make it even more watchable. Insert editing also permits new audio to be added over existing video, and vice versa.

Not all machine-to-machine systems that incorporate insert editing, especially those that are manually operated, are frame accurate despite the most careful planning and execution on your part. To ensure better accuracy, you will need some auxiliary equipment such as an *editor controller*, a valuable tool that is fed information from both the playback (source) and record (master) machines and processes it into an edited product on a master videotape. This equipment allows the editor a choice between assemble or insert editing, although once you become accustomed to insert editing, it is doubtful that you would consider the other type. Editor controllers are manufactured at varying levels of sophistication and price, but the addition of such equipment definitely enhances your editing experience.

Digital Editing   As you become more and more experienced with the editing process and look toward even more sophisticated postproduction results, many other "bells and whistles" can be added to the equipment list as the production quality and style demand, and budget allows. Complementary to video editing devices (editor controllers) are digital video/audio mixers that include many special effects functions that can make simple source video look professionally produced. Another auxiliary component to the controller and mixer is the character generator that allows for many different titling and text functions to be presented as supplement to or keyed (overlayed electronically) over video.

There are many types and brands of postproduction equipment, but it would be to your advantage to purchase components that are compatible to other pieces of equipment that may be in your school's inventory, although much of one company's equipment can be easily interfaced with another's with satisfactory results.

Editing is only one facet of area postproduction technology that has changed dramatically in the past decade, going from "ker-chunk"—manual editing on the fly—to highly sophisticated, multiple-source equipment that is totally computer controlled. Without getting into too much technical jargon, the major distinction in editing systems is linear versus nonlinear, and analog versus digital. The industry seems headed in the direction of the more high-tech, nonlinear digital systems because of their seamless accuracy and capacity to easily add, delete, and manipulate images.

The following are some comments from people who are aware of, have used, or are suggesting computer-assisted equipment:

There are very compelling reasons to investigate computer-controlled editors; they are easy to upgrade, they offer a variety of special features and they usually cost less than comparable stand-alone edit controllers.—Robert Nulph, *Videomaker: Desktop Video 96/97*

One way to get into digital video is to install a video capture board, edit software and gobs of RAM (often 120 megs or more) into a computer (Mac or PC). Connect this to an array of A/V spec hard drives for storage and you're ready to go!—Frank Johnson, graphic effects producer, Panagraph Strategic and Designed Marketing, Fresno, CA

I suggest you stick with a simple and (relatively) inexpensive solution such as the Avid Cinema card that is now sold as an add-on for the Performa 6400/200. This comes with very simple editing software from Avid.—Michael Dangerfield, CNN video editor, personal communication via Internet, January 14, 1997

Our tactic is to teach the techniques of nonlinear digital editing with Adobe Premier in computer labs (15 students a time) using regular old Power-Macs with basic AV level Pentium PCs. Then as students progress to other classes, or work with our daily TV newscasts they move on to the Media 100QX which uses the Vincent card, squirting out full-screen, high quality images suitable for broad (cable) cast. The key here is that the Media 100QX uses Adobe Premiere software—so students already know what they're doing—Tim Hudson, associate director, School of Journalism and Mass Communication, University of Oklahoma, personal communication via Internet, January 13, 1997

I spoke with friends in Amarillo. Their 11-year-old son. . .uses "3D Moviemaker" by Microsoft to make animated custom cartoon movies like the ones he and I created last Halloween. . .He also uses another program called "Hollywood" by Theatrix. Both are pretty cheap, like $50–100. Both run on PCs with a CD-Rom drive—Rich Tharp, video photographer/editor, Texas Department of Health, Austin, TX, personal communication, January 1997

If you are considering digital and computerized editing, it could be advantageous to learn from people who work with computers and digital equipment, perhaps colleagues who teach computer classes at your school, to familiarize yourself with the technology and stay steps ahead.

GENERATIONS OF VIDEOTAPE

Each time the insert editing process is used, the material being recorded on the master tape becomes another generation removed from the original video, losing some of the resolution, or detail, of the source tape. If the edit master tape is then dubbed, or copied, onto yet another videotape, it becomes the next generation, and so forth. Improvement in videotape stock and upgrading of formats, such as S-VHS, Hi-8, and, more recently, VHSC and S-VHSC, have made this less of a postproduction concern over the past few years.

STORING AND ORGANIZING TAPES

For video to be used effectively in the classroom, the tapes must be clearly labeled and a system developed for storing them, so that they are available for student and parent use. Each student may have an individual tape that is being added to in an ongoing manner throughout the year. These tapes should be stored in alphabetical order on a shelf where the students can reach them, view them, or bring them to their taping sessions. Other tapes might highlight collaborative activities and group projects. These tapes should be clearly labeled so that they can be used for parent conferences or meetings. Students may also want to include clips from these group tapes on their individual video portfolio tape.

Transferring segments from one video tape to another involves the use of a videocassette player connected by a cable to another cassette player or camcorder. The tape to be copied is played on one machine and recorded on the target tape. This process makes it possible to move taped segments onto several students' individual tapes. It also enables the teacher to do some editing without expensive editing equipment.

VIDEO PRODUCTION BIBLIOGRAPHY

Burrows, T. D., Gross, L.S., and Wood, D. N. (1995). *Television Production: Disciplines and Techniques.* Dubuque, IA: William C. Brown & Benchmark.

Cartwright, S. R., (1986). *Training with Video.* White Plains, NY: Knowledge Industry Publications, Inc.

Compesi, R. J., and Sherriffs, R. E. (1985). *Small Format Television Production: The Technique of Single-Camera Television Field Production.* Boston, MA: Allyn and Bacon.

Hausman, C. (1992). *Crafting the News for Electronic Media: Writing, Reporting and Producing.* Belmont, CA: Wadsworth Publishing.

Mayeux, P. E. (1985). *Writing for the Broadcast Media*. Boston, MA: Allyn and Bacon.

Millerson, G. (1992). *Video Production Handbook*. 2nd. ed. Oxford, MA: Focal Press.

Musburger, R. B. (1993). *Single Camera Video Production*. Stoneham, MA: Focal Press.

Nulph, R. (1997). Using computer-controlled video editing. *Videomaker 21*. 9–13.

Ohanian, T. A. (1993). *Digital Nonlinear Editing*. Newton, MA: Focal Press.

Utz, P. (1980). *Video User's Handbook*. Englewood Cliffs, NJ: Prentice-Hall.

Valmont, W. J. (1995). *Creating Videos for School Use*. Boston, MA: Allyn and Bacon.

Whitaker, R. (1993). *Television Production*, Mountain View, CA: Mayfield Publishing.

Wurtzel, A. (1979). *Television Production*, NY: McGraw-Hill.

Zettl, H. (1995). *Video Basics*, Belmont, CA: Wadsworth Publishing.

Teacher Resources

SOURCES FOR MUSIC AND SOUND EFFECTS

The following companies provide catalogues of copyright free music and sound effects that you can use in producing classroom video. You can call their toll-free numbers and request a price list and demonstration CD review. Most of the companies will provide the catalogue and demo CD free of charge.

Aircraft Music Library
1-800-343-2514

DeWolf Music Library
1-800-221-6713

Dimension Music and Sound Effects
1-800-634-0091

Firstcom/Music House/ Chappell's Music Library
1-800-858-8880

Fresh Music Library
1-800-545-0688

Manhattan Music Library
1-800-227-1954

Network Music and Effects Library
1-800-854-2075

PROMUSIC
1-800-322-7879

TM Century Production Library
1-800-879-2100

Valentino Production Music
1-800-223-6278

PREPRODUCTION CHECKLIST

Script Complete:
Storyboard Complete:
Props Needed:

—————————————————— ——————————————————
—————————————————— ——————————————————
—————————————————— ——————————————————
—————————————————— ——————————————————

—————————————————— ——————————————————

Equipment Needed:
Camcorder ———— Tripod ———— Microphones ————
Cables   ———— Cassette Tapes————

TELEVISION LITERACY CURRICULUM

A curriculum for teaching television literacy is available to teachers from TV Ontario by calling 1-800-331-9566. The kit includes lessons and support materials covering such topics as television talent, stereotypes, people behind the scenes, pictures, sound, storyboarding, scripting, editing, commercials, television viewing activities, and evaluating television programs.

USE OF COPYRIGHTED MATERIALS

Contrary to popular belief, using someone else's copyrighted material for educational purposes does not relieve you of having to obtain permission for its use. To use copyrighted material in written or video form legally, you must get permission from the copyright owner. Writing to the author for permission to use copyrighted material for a specific purpose, in a specific format is much more likely to result in permission than a request for blanket permission. If you are going to produce a school-based video and want to use a specific poem or song, write to the copyright owner and describe the project and proposed use of the copyrighted material. Include the title of the material, date of publication, the exact part that will be used, when it will be used, how many copies will be made, and how it will be distributed. Include a complete return address and include a self-addressed, stamped envelope (Sinofsky, 1988).

For use of materials videotaped from broadcast television, Crews (1993) suggests the following:

> The Off-Air Guidelines provide that nonprofit educational institutions may record television programs that are transmitted without charge to the general public. The tapes may be retained for no more than forty-five days, and may be used only once for teaching purposes during the first ten "school days" of that forty-five day retention period. One "reinforcement" use of a tape is permitted, with further uses limited to evaluation for future needs. Additional rules prohibit alterations of the programs or their reconstruction into "anthologies." The guidelines also limit teachers to one recording of a program, even if it may be broadcast repeatedly. The implications are clear: if repeated uses are anticipated, or if the use is more than ten "school days" into the future, teachers must seek permission from copyright owners before taping, retaining, or using the television program.

AN INEXPENSIVE CONNECTION BETWEEN CAMCORDER AND MICROSCOPE

A piece of black craft foam or construction paper fashioned into a funnel and held in place with tape serves as an inexpensive connection between the camcorder and a microscope. The small end of the funnel is placed over the microscope eyepiece with the larger end of the funnel used to shield the camcorder lens from outside light.

With the camcorder connected directly to a television monitor, the microscope view is shown on the screen where it is easily viewed by the whole class. See the *Camcorder in the Classroom* video for a demonstration of this strategy.

VIDEO INFORMATION

The following may be helpful:
The Video Encyclopedia of the 20th Century
CEL Educational Resources
1-800-235-3339

The *Video Encyclopedia of the 20th Century* includes:
44 Videodiscs
2 copies of cross-referenced index volume
4-volume reference set
2 index and reference update books
1 set of user's guides and curriculum materials

Vocabulary Enterprises
What's the Word?
1-888-44LEARN
www.easylearn.com

REFERENCES

Crews, Kenneth D. (1993). *Copyright, Fair Use and the Challenge for Universities*. Chicago, IL: The University of Chicago Press.
Sinofsky, E. (1988). *A Copyright Primer for Educational and Industrial Media Producers*. Friday Harbor, WA: Copyright Information Services.

acquisition format   A small, inexpensive VCR format used to tape video footage that later will be copied to a higher-quality format before editing. This procedure minimizes loss of quality during the editing procedure.

adapter   A device used to achieve compatibility between two pieces of audiovisual equipment

advance organizer   A teaching strategy used to give students information in advance so they can participate more successfully in a lesson.

amplitude   The measurement of the loudness or intensity of sound.

animation   Single shots of video, illustrations, drawings, or photographs that create an illusion of movement when put together in sequence. Computer-generated animation has speeded up the process greatly and has enhanced quality.

announcer (ANNCR)   An individual, either on- or off-camera, who provides oral explanation of the contents of the video; script abbreviation for announcer. *see also:* narrator.

aspect ratio   The relationship of the height of a television picture to its width. The standard broadcast aspect ratio is 3×4 (3 units high by 4 units wide, or 3:4).

assemble editing   The process of postproduction of adding a new video or audio sequence to a previously taped scene, creating a new control track.

audio board   An electronic console used to control and mix sound levels from multiple sources.

audio dub   A copy of a previously recorded audio segment. Also, an editing technique that involves erasing the previously taped audio track and replacing it with a new audio track.

audio sweetening   A post production process designed to correct problems in audio as well as to enhance and supplement audio tracks.

audio/video mixer   A single electronic device that consists of an audio mixer and a video mixer, switcher, or special effects generator.

author's chair   A chair in the classroom reserved for students to sit and read completed writing aloud to the class.

axis   An imaginary line, one side on which cameras must stay to avoid jump cuts and incorrect screen positions of subjects during production.

backlight (backlight switch)   A light focused from behind and above a subject used to separate the subject form the background and to add illumination to the head and shoulders; also a feature on some camcorders to compensate for strong light behind a subject when the camera is in front of the subject.

Back-to-School Night   A meeting for parents held at the beginning of the school year. Teachers introduce themselves and provide information about their plans for the school year.

Betacam   A broadcast-quality videocassette format that uses ½ inch videotape.

book commercial   An oral presentation in which a student gives information about a book in an attempt to interest other students in reading the book.

broadcast quality   Equipment or production that conforms to the highest-quality technical standards. Originally, the Federal Communications Commission established many of these standards.

camcorder   An all-in-one *camera* and re*corder*.

camera operator   A person who operates and controls a video camera in either a studio or on remote locations.

CCD (charge-coupled device)   An electronic element that converts optical images into video signals.

CCU (Camera control unit)   An electronic component to control and adjust video elements.

character generator (CG)   A video component that provides a way to type words and graphics onto the video screen.

clip-on   A small, unobtrusive microphone that can be attached to clothing.

close-up   A video shot framed tightly on a face or an object to show expression or detail.

collaborative group   A teaching strategy in which two to five students work together. Each student has an assigned job.

composition The selection and arrangement of images within shots to provide the maximum aesthetic and technical effects desired.

consumer quality A popular but unofficial classification of video and audio equipment quality that ranks below industrial and broadcast quality.

continuity A process of ensuring accuracy and consistency in the relationship of shots, props, screen direction and position, talent, dialog, and other elements of a production. Electronic pulses recorded onto videotape that help stabilize and synchronize video signals; essential in linear insert editing.

control track Electronic pulses recorded onto videotape that help stabilize and synchronize video signals; essential in linear insert editing.

cover shot Usually a wide or long shot of a scene that establishes the relationship of important elements in the scene; also used to cover errors with lip sync or action that does not match from one point to another.

crawl Graphics that move across the television screen, usually at the bottom; for example: a weather alert.

CU Abbreviation and script reference for a close-up shot.

culminating activities In teaching, activities that celebrate the conclusion of a unit of study.

cut An instantaneous change form one video shot to another; a take; also refers to taking out unwanted audio or video material in a production.

cutaway A brief shot inserted during the main action to reinforce an audio or visual reference.

depth of field The area in a scene that remains in focus from a point nearest the camera to a point farthest form the camera.

diffusion In lighting, the use of a device or material to soften light. Diffusers are used in conjunction with camera lenses to soften images.

director The person responsible for all elements and activities during a production.

dissolve A video transition in which one video signal is gradually replaced by another as their images overlap; generally used to show change of place or time, in musical or entertainment presentations, or fantasy and dream sequences.

docudrama A production based on real persons or events and presented in a dramatic format.

documentary approach A reality-based approach to production content, generally on a specific topic, that more closely follows a news presentation format than a dramatic format.

dolly (in or out) The forward or backward movement of the camera and its mount; also, a piece of mobile equipment used to support a production camera.

ECU Extreme close-up shot; generally showing a person's face from the forehead to the bottom on the chin.

edit The modification or removal of previously recorded video or audio material.

edit controller A device from which two or more editing machines are controlled during the editing process; used to program and control the editing process.

edit(ed) master The tape on which the final video an audio segments will be electronically recorded.

editing The process of selecting and arranging video and audio material in a specific sequence.

editor A person who edits; an electronic device that performs video and audio editing.

emergent reader A child still learning to read.

emergent writer A child still learning to write.

establishing shot An initial wide shot that introduces and relates all elements of a scene to the audience.

executive producer A person often responsible for a number of programs in production at one time, usually the person in charge of budgeting, scheduling, and creative aspects.

EXT Script designation for exterior, used to describe scenes in film-style scripts.

fade A video technique in which the picture is gradually replaced (up) from or to black, or a background color.

floor manager Person responsible for the studio during production; the director's main communication link form the control room to the studio.

fluid head A type of panning device on which the camera is positioned. The fluid head is named for a liquid (often silicon) that allows for smooth tilt and pan movements of heavier cameras.*See* friction head.

flying (erase) head A video head that engages when the video deck is on pause providing a clear still-frame image.

follow focus   A feature that allows the focus on the camera to be adjusted while following a moving subject.

frequency   The repetition of a sound wave during a given time period.

friction head   A type of camera panning head controlled by friction of its moving parts; not as smooth as fluid head mounts.

gel   A sheet of translucent material placed over a light to change the color or diffuse the light.

grand conversation   A discussion of literature conducted when a group of people had completed reading a section or whole book. May be focused on a particular element of the story.

group interaction skills   Conversation and participation skills that contribute to successful group dynamics.

head   Electromagnet that records video and audio signals onto videotape.

head clog   A loss of video signal resulting from dirt in the microscopic gap of a video head.

head room   The a small area of background that shows above the head of the subject in framing for a video shot.

Hi8 (hi-band 8mm)   High-quality Sony videotape that contains metal particles.

industrial   An audio and video equipment quality designation that falls between **broadcast quality** and **consumer quality.**

insert editing   As opposed to **assemble editing,** an editing process that inserts video and audio information over an existing control track and/or previously recorded audio/video material.

interview format   The use of a basic interview as the basis of production or program segment.

intrapersonal intelligence   One of the seven intelligences. People who have strong intrapersonal intelligence knows their own strengths and thought processes.

intro   Introduction. The initial or beginning elements of a program or production.

iris   A diaphragm that can be adjusted to control light as it enters a camera lens.

jump cut   An obvious and unattractive transition between two shots of similar size, a change in screen position of subjects, or a segment whose middle appears to have been disjoined.

key   An effect in which a video source is electronically inserted into background video.

key light   Refers to the lighting instrument and lighting position used to illuminate a subject from a frontal angle.

kinesthetic intelligence   One of the seven intelligences. People who have strong kinesthetic intelligence remember actions made by the body and mimic actions easily.

lavaliere; lav mike   A small microphone that can be clipped on to clothing or hung from a neck strap or cord.

lead room (nose room)   Space in front, and in the direction, of moving object in a video scene or frame.

lecture format   A production or program-segment approach that features an individual communicating information directly to a camera, in somewhat the same manner as a teacher addresses a class.

lens shade (lens hood)   A shield that fits over the end of a camera lens to prevent unwanted light from reaching the lens.

linear editing   A procedure that requires editing from beginning to end. Changes necessitate rerecording all material that followed the edit point. *See* nonlinear editing.

linguistic intelligence   One of the seven intelligences. People who have strong linguistic intelligence use language to explain and solve problems well.

lip sync   The mouthing of words as they are being played synchronously from a prerecorded sound track.

literature discussion group   A group of people who get together to discuss a piece of writing that they have read.

logging   Identifying all raw footage from the order shot on individual videotapes. A log should include the beginning and end times for each segment, a brief description of content, and whether or not the shot is usable.

logical-mathematical intelligence   One of the seven intelligences. People who has strong logical-mathematical intelligence use math and logic to solve problems easily.

LS   In scripts, an abbreviation for long shot.

macro lens   A lens designed to shoot close-ups of small objects; usually a part of the lens component on the camera.

master shot   A wide shot in which all major elements are seen and which become the reference shot for other video, such as close-up shots.

MCU   Script designation for medium close-up.

medium shot (MS)   Object seen from a medium distance. Normally covers framing between a long shot and a close-up.

mike   Microphone; the device that detects sound and changes it into electrical energy.

MLS   Script designation for medium long shot.

montage   A sequence of brief video scenes arranged to give an impression or convey a story.

MS   Script designation for medium shot.

multiple intelligences   A theory credited to Howard Gardner that identifies seven different intelligences: interpersonal, intrapersonal, kinesthetic, linguistic, logical-mathematical, musical, and spatial.

musical intelligence   One of the seven intelligences. People who have strong musical intelligence remember melody, rhythm, and rhyme easily and learn well when information is presented in musical or rhythmic ways.

narrator   An individual, usually off-camera, who provides narration for a production NARR is the script abbreviation for narrator.

noise   Unwanted interference in video or audio signals. Video noise is generally snow or graininess; audio noise is static, buzzing, or hissing sounds.

nonlinear editing   A procedure by which video can be ordered in any sequence at any time and can be altered at any point on the master tape without affecting material before or after the edit point; usually associated with computer-assisted editing.

nose room (lead room)   Screen space in front of a moving subject.

on-line (editing)   Sophisticated editing process that combines multiple video and audio sources through computer-assisted equipment and places them on the master tape. *See* nonlinear editing.

OSV   Abbreviation and script reference for off-screen voice.

over-the-shoulder (OTS; OS) shot   Usually a two-shot taken over the shoulder of one person and focusing on the reaction and expression of the other; *reverse OTS* simply switches the angle, shooting over the shoulder of the other subject.

pan handle   The handle extending from the pan head that is used to control panning and tilting movement of the camera.

pan head   The connecting device that attaches the camera to the camera mount and allows horizontal (pan) and vertical (tilt) movements of the camera.

pan (panning)   The horizontal movement of the camera head left or right, usually from a stationary position on a tripod or pedestal.

parallel cutting   Cutting back and forth between two or more related stories in a dramatic production.

pedestal   The center post of a tripod that can be adjusted up or down; a piece of heavy mobile equipment on which a studio camera is mounted and can be raised and lowered; an engineering term indicating measurement and calibration of video black level.

point of view (POV)   A shot in which the camera becomes subjective, much like a participant in the scene.

portfolio   A collection of a person's best work. It may be composed of drawings, photographs, writing, or almost any combination of work.

postproduction phase   The final phase in a production, including follow-up and evaluation. Typically, postproduction is mainly seen as the editing phase.

preproduction phase   The all-important, initial planning phase in production; all work that precedes the actual production.

producer   The person(s) responsible for developing and organizing all aspects of a production, including financing, hiring cast, crew, and production staff, and for some, if not all, of the creative aspects.

producer-director   An individual who takes on the role of both producer and director in a production, the individual with the primary responsibility for guiding the production through all production phases.

production phase   As opposed to the preproduction and postproduction phases, the interval during which the actual video and audio are recorded or (in the case of live production) broadcast.

rack focus   A transition technique that shifts focus from one subject/object/location to another, generally in response to a changing point of interest in a scene. The camera moves in on a subject while defocusing; the subject changes during this interval and the camera moves back out while refocusing to reveal the new subject, object, or location.

random scribbling Marks on paper characterized by lack of control, usually by a small child.

rap Lyrics performed to rhythm rather than music, characterized by a strong beat.

raw footage All unedited audio and video taped during the production process.

reaction shot A shot of a person's expression in response to something just said or done; a cutaway shot.

reader's theater A dramatic production of a script by a group of readers who interpret the script by reading with expression using few props.

reading/writing workshop A block of time set aside in the school day in which students are actively involved in reading and writing self-selected books and topics.

resolution The measurement of clarity and detail that a camera system can reproduce.

rubric A set of standards used to assess performance, usually on a numeric scale.

rule of thirds A guideline in composition based on placing the center of interest at or near the intersecting points of two equally spaced horizontal and two equally spaced vertical lines in the image area.

scheduling Breaking down scenes based on shooting sites, crew, talent, props, etc. for a more efficient shooting guideline or timetable.

script Sometimes called the "spine" of a production, contains essential information about a story's time, place, characters, and dialog and eventually will include camera shots and movements.

selective focus A technique that uses shallow depth of field to draw attention to some parts of a scene.

SFX Abbreviation for special audio or video effects.

shot The basic visual element that contains information important to the storyline of a production. A series of shots in a continuous sequence gives meaning and logic to action and events being viewed.

shotgun microphone A microphone with an extremely focused directional pickup pattern.

slate A visual that gives information about a scene to be shot, such as date, time, take number, script page, and director. This helps in locating and identifying segments used in the preedit logging process.

snap zoom A fast zoom from a wide shot to a close-up shot of a subject that can influence the pacing of a program.

snow A scrambled, grainy effect caused by noise or absence of a video image.

sound bite A selected voice segment from a (usually) longer statement that has immediacy, clarity, and newsworthiness.

sound on tape (SOT) Videotape that includes a sound track.

sound/symbol relationship Using letters to represent sounds in writing.

spatial intelligence One of the seven intelligences. People with strong spatial intelligence are attuned to the position of objects in space and represent things well visually.

storyboards A series of rough sketches of scenes and shots that help visualize the elements and continuity of the script.

strobe (stroboscopic) effect A series of quick images of a motion, usually the result of using an electronic device that is part of a video camera. Also a pulsating light the speed of which can be regulated.

super VHS (S-VHS) A videotape format based on VHS but with a wider luminance bandwidth; has a potential horizontal resolution of more than 400 lines and allows component recording and playback without cross-luminance or cross-color artifacts.

swish pan The very rapid horizontal movement of a camcorder that produces a blurred image, used as a transitional device.

switcher An electronic video component that allows a technician to perform cuts, wipes, dissolves, and fades selecting from several video sources; also, the operator who performs the functions on a switcher.

take (cut) An immediate change form one shot to another or from one camera or video source to another; often many takes are recorded for later selection of the best during postproduction.

talent A person or persons who perform in front of the camera.

talent release (form) A legal permission form signed by talent granting rights to a producer or production company to broadcast the subject's image and/or voice.

tally light   The red light on a video camera that indicates the camera is on air or that videotape is recording the image it is shooting.

three-shot   A video picture containing three individuals.

tighten up   Director's command to move in closer to a subject with a zoom or dolly.

tilt (tilting)   The vertical, up-and-down movement of the camera on the pan head, usually from a stationary position on a tripod or pedestal.

timing   The total length of a production, including time allotted to the individual scenes and program components.

tracking (control)   Adjustment of video heads to align with invisible magnetic video information tracks on videotape to keep the picture stabilized.

tracking shot (travel shot)   A shot that moves along with a subject or moves in relationship to a stationary subject. *See* truck shot.

treatment   A brief outline or summary of a proposed program or series that includes the basic premise, description of characters, production methods, a sample of dialog, etc.; is generally presented to a producer, production company, or network in hopes that it will be accepted, financed, and produced for broadcast.

tripod ("sticks")   A three-legged device on which a camera is mounted for support, has a pan head, handle, and adjustable legs and usually can be raised and lowered ("pedded up"); sometimes can be converted with wheels for more mobility.

truck   Right or left movement of the camera on its mount parallel to action or subject.

TV receiver   A television set that can be tuned to pick up video channels and reproduce image and sound.

two-shot   A picture showing two persons or objects.

VCR   Videocassette recorder (as compared to VTR-videotape recorder).

VHS-C   A compact version of VHS. Resolution is approximately 400 lines.

VHS (video home system)   A consumer-level videotape format using $\frac{1}{2}$-inch tape in a cassette. Resolution is approximately 250 lines.

Video gain switch   A control on the camera that allows a boost in the video signal; often used in low light situations but can make the video quality noisy or dull and grainy.

video monitor   A television set that displays video and audio but cannot be tuned to video channels.

viewfinder   A small TV screen built into the camera that helps the camera operator to frame shots before and during recording; also used to see playback of recorded video in the camera. Information modules in the viewfinder display the status of the camera battery, how much tape has been used is remaining, and light level conditions.

VLS   Abbreviation and script reference for very long shot.

voice over (VO)   Off-camera narration.

VTR   Videotape recorder (as compared to VCR—videocassette recorder).

wide shot (WS)   Abbreviation and script reference for wide shot. (*See:* establishing shot).

wipe   A transitional effect by which one full-screen image is gradually—or quickly—replaced by another full-screen image; also can introduce wipe effect patterns with soft or hard edges gradually or quickly over a video background.

yo-yo shots ("see-saw" shots)   Excessive, repetitive zooming in and out on a subject.

zooming (in and out)   Changing the focal length and, therefore, the size of the image with varying speeds while the camera is stationary. Generally, the zoom lens is operated by buttons on the camera marked T for tight, and W for wide.

zoom lens   A variable focal length lens.

Z-axis   Imaginary line that extends form the camera "through" a subject and to the horizon. Objects placed along the axis provide depth with distinctive foreground, middle ground, and background points.